Veg Out
Vegetarian Guide® to
Chicago

Coming Fall 2005!

VegOut:
Vegetarian
Guide® to
Houston
$12.95
Paperback
1-58685-396-1

VegOut:
Vegetarian
Guide® to
Miami/Ft. Lauderdale
$12.95
Paperback
1-58685-394-5

Veg Out

Vegetarian Guide® to Chicago

Margaret Littman

Gibbs Smith, Publisher
Salt Lake City

First Edition
09 08 07 06 05   5 4 3 2 1

© 2005 Margaret Littman

All rights reserved. No part of this book may be reproduced by any means whatsoever without written permission from the publisher, except brief portions quoted for purpose of review.

Published by
Gibbs Smith, Publisher
P.O. Box 667
Layton, Utah 84041

Orders: 1-800-748-5439
www.gibbs-smith.com

Cover design by Kurt Wahlner
Interior design by Frederick Schneider/Grafis
Printed and bound in China

Library of Congress Cataloging-in-Publication Data

Littman, Margaret.
VegOut : vegetarian guide to Chicago / by Margaret Littman.— 1st ed.
p. cm.
Includes indexes.
ISBN 1-58685-384-8
1. Vegetarian restaurants—Illinois—Chicago—Guidebooks. I. Title.
TX907.3.I32C4725 2005
647.95773'11—dc22
                              2004021364

Contents

Foreword 6
Preface 7
Acknowledgments 9
About This Book 11
Restaurants 13
    North Side 13
    Downtown 85
    South Side 119
    Suburban Cook County 135
    Collar Counties: DuPage, Kane, Lake,
        McHenry, Will 159
Resources 173
Community-Supported Agriculture 175
Juice Bars 177
Farmers Markets 181
Green Grocers and Health Food Stores . 186
Indexes 193
    Alphabetical Index 193
    Cuisine Index 195
    Top 10 Index 199

Foreword

Gibbs Smith, Publisher, is thrilled to present a series of vegetarian and vegan guides to major cities and regions throughout the United States and the world. Our primary goal is to have the guides be useful to consumers as they explore their own communities and travel near and far in search of the finest quality vegetarian and vegan fare.

We also hope to encourage and celebrate established vegetarian and vegan communities and to invite their exploration by many more people. Our objective is to further the pleasurable and health-giving effects of vegetarian and vegan dining.

We encourage you to use the guides and to be part of the creation of future guides in the series, as we revise and update each edition. As you discover new or established vegetarian or vegan restaurants that deserve the attention of others, please let us know. Either e-mail us at vegout@gibbs-smith.com or fill out and mail us the reply card found in the front of this book. If your recommended restaurant is chosen for an upcoming edition of *VegOut*, we'll send you a free copy of that new edition.

Happy eating!

Preface

To write a book about vegetarian restaurants in a city known as "hog butcher to the world" may seem like a fool's errand. But after dining at more than 200 veg-friendly eateries—ranging from those with Formica countertops to those with Gold Coast white tablecloths—I learned that the truly foolish are those who write off vegetarian as a culinary afterthought. My quest for meat-free menus introduced me to several new cravings, from Long Life Thai Noodles to chickpea french fries to vegan cornbread and collard greens, not to mention more varieties of Indian pakora than I previously knew existed.

Such new cravings fit my gastronomic past. While many eaters shied away from vegetables as kids, I gravitated toward them. Instead, it is the dishes that most resemble our animal friends—chicken on the bone, fish with heads attached, those creepy black eyes looking up from shrimp—that have always made me squirm.

While my tastes have matured a little over the years, I found researching *VegOut! Vegetarian Guide to Chicago* to be a culinary dream come true: heavy on the polenta and lentils, and not one pork shoulder in sight.

As a journalist and editor with a specialty in food, nutrition, and restaurant writing, I wrote *VegOut! Vegetarian Guide to Chicago* as my second niche guidebook to my adopted home, having written *The Dog Lover's Companion to Chicago* in 2003. (While my springer spaniel, Natasha, didn't enjoy researching my book without meat as much as she enjoyed sniffing out dog parks, she happily indulged in the contents of plenty of doggy bags filled with vegetarian lasagna, naan, and baba ghanooj.)

With both books, I've learned that the cliché of Chicago as a city of neighborhoods exists because it is true. It's even more accurate when it comes to eating out vegetarian-style, with pockets of ethnic neighborhoods offering some of the best, most interesting, and most authentic meat-free fare. Like Chicago's always-impressive restaurant scene, the selection of veg-friendly eateries run the gamut from greasy corner diners to upscale bistros with attentive sommeliers. Some of the area's most acclaimed chefs, including Suzy Crofton, Shawn McClain, and Michael Taus, are devoting more than half of their kitchens to developing innovative dishes focusing on locally grown seasonal produce rather than meat. Not that a culinary degree is required. In Chicago, there are plenty of veg-friendly options for the Big Shoulders crowd. That means plenty of quick meat-free bites, albeit sometimes not so healthy but, of course, still tasty.

So, dig in and show Carl Sandburg the veg-friendly side of the city he left unexplored.

—Margaret Littman

Acknowledgments

As much as anyone loves to eat (and, boy, do I love to eat), writing a guidebook requires more than one stomach and one set of tastebuds. Thanks to Cat Auer, Sharon Bloyd-Peskin, Kelly James-Enger, Priya Khatkhate, Paul Rogers, Jennifer Rothschild, Jason Rothstein, Judy Sutton Taylor, Christine Tyler, and Karla Zimmerman. Their tireless crisscrossing of the Kennedy Expressway and Roosevelt Road to review the city's and suburbs' best—and their ability to write about them well—is what made this guide possible.

In addition to reviewing many of the downtown lunchtime locales, Elisa Kronish took on the nearly impossible task of fact checking the data we all gathered along with our doggy bags, take-out menus, and receipts. While she and I took care to verify all the information in this book, sensible diners will call ahead. Restaurants routinely change their menus, change their hours, and close their doors in the time it takes your sag paneer to get cold.

Thanks, as always, to my friends, family, and editors—particularly the carnivores—who tolerated eight months of my singular focus, and my arrogant insistence that if they wanted to spend time with me, it had to be at one of the places on "The List." An extra acknowledgment to Bev Bennett, without whom I never would have become a book author in the first place, nor would I have taken this veggie adventure.

Final thanks to Jennifer Grillone, Linda Nimori, Alison Einerson, Toni Apgar, and the Gibbs Smith, Publisher staff for their editing, ideas, and support.

About This Book

This guide is straightforward and easy to use. Each restaurant entry has a rating for food and cost and a description of the atmosphere. It also includes a review and other pertinent information such as hours, types of payment accepted, parking, and alcohol availability. Food and cost rating keys are listed below.

Food in each restaurant is rated as follows:

★	Fair
★★	Good
★★★	Excellent
★★★★	Outstanding

Cost for each restaurant is rated as follows:

$	Inexpensive (under $10)
$$	Moderate ($10 to $20)
$$$	Expensive ($21 and above)

The cost includes the price for an entrée, plus one drink and tip.

For the purposes of this guide, *vegetarian* means food that is prepared without any meat products; *vegan* means food prepared without meat or dairy products. A note at the bottom of each restaurant listing indicates what kind of food is served in the restaurant. Not every restaurant in the book is strictly vegetarian. Some restaurants with full menus were also included if the vegetarian offerings were ample or if the restaurants were veg-friendly.

NOTE: Vegetarian and vegan can mean many things to many people. The stricter your diet, the more sense it makes to ask before you eat.

Restaurants

North Side

★★ / $$
1. A La Turka: Turkish Kitchen

3134 North Lincoln Avenue
Chicago, IL 60657
773.935.6101
www.turkishkitchen.us

TURKISH

Hours:	Sun-Wed noon to 11:00 p.m.
	Th-Sat noon to 1:00 a.m.
Payment:	Credit cards accepted
Parking:	Ample metered street parking
Alcohol:	Full bar
Atmosphere:	"I Dream of Jeanie" casual

Between the colorful surroundings, the expansive menu, the choice of chairs or pillows, and (on weekends) the belly dancing, there's a lot for a first-time visitor to A La Turka to absorb. With so much sensory input, you might be tempted to go with the Middle Eastern standards on the menu, but if you look a little deeper, you'll find many more interesting things from which to choose. Ezme, roasted red peppers crushed with tomatoes, onions, and walnuts, is a popular starter, as are the eggplant dip and the zucchini pancake with carrots and feta cheese ($6 to $6.50). And there are few things more refreshing than cazik, a cold yogurt-and-cucumber soup with garlic and mint ($4). Entrée portions include tasty choices like stuffed baby eggplant with onions, peppers, and cheese with tomato sauce, or Turkish macaroni, loaded with vegetables and covered in tomato sauce and mozzarella ($13 to $16). Spinach and vegetable options are available for the Turkish wraps offered at lunchtime, which are served on homemade lavash (sesame bread). Finish up with baklava and Turkish coffee or tea; or if you prefer a different kind of relaxation, order up the hookah (water pipe) with some apple-flavored tobacco ($15).

FULL MENU WITH MANY VEGETARIAN OPTIONS

★ / $$
2. Abhiruchi

> 2544 West Devon Avenue
> Chicago, IL 60659
> 773.262.1450
>
> **SOUTH INDIAN**
>
> | | |
> |---|---|
> | *Hours:* | Mon, Wed-Sun 11:30 a.m. to 10:00 p.m. Closed Tue |
> | *Payment:* | Credit cards accepted |
> | *Parking:* | Metered street parking, can be challenging on weekends |
> | *Alcohol:* | BYO, no corkage fee |
> | *Atmosphere:* | Midscale |

Blazing orange walls foreshadow what your mouth feels like after indulging in the pleasurable pain of the chili-laced uttapam (savory pancake). Kindly servers explain the various chutneys, sambhar, and other sauces, some of which cool the fire. The ten-table restaurant has an equally small menu with four vegetarian entrées ($7.95 each): korma (veggies and coconut milk), bhindi masala (okra), palak paneer (cheese and spinach), and eggplant curry. Besides the offbeat egg pakoda (boiled egg battered and deep fried, $3.50), Abhiruchi serves the usual array of tasty Indian appetizers (idli, vada, and samosas), dosas, and breads. While not a standout in terms of price or taste, Abhiruchi is one of Devon Avenue's many solid veg-friendly options. Appetizers $2 to $6, entrées about $8 each.

FULL MENU WITH MANY VEGETARIAN OFFERINGS

★★★ / $$
3. Addis Abeba

>3521 North Clark Street
>Chicago, IL 60657
>773.929.9383
>
>**ETHIOPIAN**
>
>| | |
>|---|---|
>| **Hours:** | Mon-Sat 5:00 p.m. to 10:00 p.m. |
>| | Sun 4:00 p.m. to 10:00 p.m. |
>| **Payment:** | Credit cards accepted |
>| **Parking:** | Street parking, can be challenging on weekend nights and whenever there is a Cubs game; least expensive pay lot is on Addison Street just west of Clark Street (behind the Cubby Bear) |
>| **Alcohol:** | Full bar |
>| **Atmosphere:** | Midscale |

Foamy pieces of flat, sour injera bread serve as knife, fork, and spoon to scoop up the twelve vegetarian entrées ($6.50 to $9.25). A good way to sample is via the veg combo ($11.50), where diners choose four dishes. One combo can suffice for two timid eaters, but it's best for heartier eaters to get their own. Choices include timatim fitfit (injera pieces sautéed in jalapeno, onion, and tomatoes), azifa (cold lentils, tomatoes, and jalapeno seasoned with ginger, garlic, lemon, and olive oil), and yeater kit wot (stew with yellow split peas cooked with garlic, cloves, and cinnamon). The spices in the sambusa appetizer, a lentil-stuffed fried dough pocket, taste fresh-ground. Sambusas are available on weekends only. Tej, a traditional sweet honey wine, smoothes the injera's tang. Colorful Ethiopian folk art and carvings decorate the walls, making Wrigley's ivy-covered outfield seem worlds away.

FULL MENU WITH MANY VEGETARIAN OFFERINGS

★★ / $$
4. Alice and Friends' Vegetarian Cafe

5812 North Broadway
Chicago, IL 60660
773.275.8797

ECLECTIC ASIAN

Hours:	*Mon-Fri 4:00 to 10:00 p.m.*
	Sat noon to 9:00 p.m.
	Closed Sun
Payment:	*Credit cards accepted*
Parking:	*Ample street parking*
Alcohol:	*None*
Atmosphere:	*Small, funky, college-like cafe*

With its lavender walls, hanging tapestries, bulletin boards, classical music, and young clientele, Alice and Friends' feels like a college-town coffee shop. But the quiet, two-room Uptown restaurant actually offers a full, almost entirely vegan Asian menu. The focus of the main dishes is vegan versions of meat-based items. Don't miss the smoked veggie duck, which features slices of seitan (wheat gluten) that look and taste like poultry, or the Korean-style barbeque ($6.99), a stir-fry of beef-like seitan with broccoli and crisp rice threads. The bi bim bop ($6.99), a Korean dish of rice covered with mushroom, tofu, and vegetables, is delicious and creatively includes bright yellow sprouts as a nod to the missing egg. Recommended appetizers include tofu and mushroom dumplings (six for $3.99) and "In the Name of Love," an artful salad of beets and lightly grilled tofu over crispy lettuce with an orange sauce ($5.99). The shakes, fruit smoothies, hot and cold teas, and juices are popular, but desserts are unremarkable.

VEGETARIAN MENU WITH MANY VEGAN ITEMS

★★ / $$
5. Amarind's

> 6822 North Avenue
> Chicago, IL 60611
> 773.889.9999

> **THAI**

> | | |
> |---|---|
> | **Hours:** | Tue-Th 11:30 a.m. to 3:30 p.m., 5:00 p.m. to 9:30 p.m. |
> | | Fri-Sat 11:30 a.m. to 3:30 p.m., 5:00 p.m. to 10:00 p.m. |
> | | Sun 3:00 p.m. to 9:00 p.m. |
> | | Closed Mon |
> | **Payment:** | Credit cards accepted |
> | **Parking:** | Free lot in back |
> | **Alcohol:** | Beer and wine |
> | **Atmosphere:** | Kid-friendly, neighborhood Thai |

Kids like the castle-looking building and the chopsticks. Adults like the fact that chef/owner Rangsan Sutcharit—a veteran of Albany Park's award-winning Arun's—offers high-end, vegetarian-friendly Thai food at typically inexpensive Thai-restaurant prices. The menu includes fairly traditional offerings, with vegetarian standouts like pad thai as well as less-expected but equally tasty choices such as spinach noodles and chive dumplings served with a spicy chili soy sauce. Amarind's, which is at the edge of Chicago near the suburb of Oak Park, can be loud, and on weekends, waits can be long; so plan your trip when you're not in a rush to be somewhere else.

FULL MENU WITH MANY VEGETARIAN OFFERINGS

★★★ / $$$
6. Ambria

> 2300 North Lincoln Park West
> Chicago IL, 60614
> 773.472.5959
>
> **SEASONAL FRENCH**
>
> | | |
> |---|---|
> | *Hours:* | Mon-Fri 6:00 p.m. to 10:00 p.m. |
> | | Sat 5:00 p.m. to 10:30 p.m. |
> | | Closed Sun |
> | *Payment:* | Credit cards |
> | *Parking:* | Street parking difficult, valet |
> | *Alcohol:* | Full bar |
> | *Atmosphere:* | Upscale, jacket-required romantic restaurant |

Plenty of high-end restaurants offer a vegetarian prix fixe menu. Fewer offer one that is ordered as often by carnivores as by vegetarians. At Ambria, the $75 multicourse vegetarian degustation changes with the seasons. But what doesn't change is that the menu is extraordinary, with dishes such as leek risotto, open-face ravioli, white asparagus, sunchoke soup, and fava beans with seared porcini mushrooms. As expected at these prices, no detail is overlooked. The sommelier is chatty and willing to work with new enophiles. The wood-paneled room is decorated with white tablecloths, fresh flowers, and plenty of mirrors, creating an atmosphere that makes this Lincoln Park restaurant one of the city's most romantic. The degustation includes dessert, so you have no excuse not to try the chocolate soufflé or the passion fruit soup (so good, even chocolate addicts don't miss the lack of cocoa).

**A LA CARTE AND PRIX FIXE
VEGETARIAN MENU OPTIONS**

NORTH SIDE

★★ / $$
7. Amitabul

6207 North Milwaukee Avenue
Chicago, IL 60646
773.774.0276

KOREAN/BUDDHIST

Hours:	Tue-Th 1:00 p.m. to 9:00 p.m.
	Fri noon to 10:00 p.m.
	Sat 10:00 a.m. to 10:00 p.m.
	Sun 10:00 a.m. to 8:00 p.m.
Payment:	Credit cards accepted
Parking:	Ample street parking
Alcohol:	No
Atmosphere:	Casual

Although seemingly a little out of place on this stretch of North Milwaukee Avenue, chefs Bill and Dave nonetheless draw enthusiastic pilgrims from all over the city to their tranquil and tasty outpost in the Forrest Glen neighborhood. Amitabul, whose name translates roughly to "Awaken," features a primarily Korean menu with Tibetan and Indonesian influences. Starters include favorites like dumplings and generous portions of vegan maki rolls ($7 to $8). Meatless versions of Korean favorites like chop chae and bi bim bop (with brown rice) are popular, but many of the real standouts on the menu are also more colorfully named: Nine Ways to Nirvana (whole-wheat noodle soup), Dark Side of the Moon (veggies with black bean miso sauce), and Dr. K's Cure-All Noodle Soup (particularly recommended for hangovers, priced from $6 to $9). For those avoiding wheat as well as meat, most noodle dishes can be prepared with rice noodles or delicious sweet potato noodles instead. One final tip: "spicy" really does mean hot here; speak up if you want a milder meal.

VEGAN

★ / $
8. Amrit Ganga

2629 West Devon Avenue
Chicago, IL 60659
773.262.5281

INDIAN

Hours:	Daily 11:00 a.m. to 9:00 p.m. Closed Tue
Payment:	Cash only
Parking:	Metered street parking, can be challenging on weekends
Alcohol:	No
Atmosphere:	Snack shop

If Archie, Veronica, and Jughead had grown up in Bombay instead of Riverdale, they probably would have hung out at Amrit Ganga instead of Pop's Malt Shoppe. This slightly quirky Indian snack and sweet shop is a great place to duck in for a quick bite (and catch up on Bollywood's latest hit songs). If you have a craving for samosa, pakora, or kulfi, you'll find flavorful versions here, but it's also fun to roll the dice and try one of the many items you've probably never heard of, either by pointing at something attractive in the case or trying to pronounce one of the specials written on the menu board (hint: it's probably fried). With few items exceeding $2, it's a small gamble to take. Although the emphasis is on small plates, there's usually a dinner special for $4.99. To pass the time you can admire the thatched roof awnings over the booths or have your fortune told by an in-house palmist ($20).

VEGETARIAN

★★★ / $$
9. Anatolian Kabob

4609 North Lincoln Avenue
Chicago, IL 60625
773.561.2200
www.anatoliankabob.com

TURKISH/MEDITERRANEAN

Hours:	Mon, Wed-Th 4:00 p.m. to 10:00 p.m.
	Fri-Sat 11:30 a.m. to 11:00 p.m.
	Sun 11:30 a.m. to 10:00 p.m.
	Closed Tue
Payment:	Credit cards accepted
Parking:	Metered street parking, pay lot one block south
Alcohol:	BYO, no corkage fee
Atmosphere:	Family-owned casual

Walking by Anatolian Kabob you might just miss it. You'd never guess that the kitchen of this twelve-table restaurant, complete with aquarium, is led by a former Palmer House hotel chef with a penchant for healthy Turkish cuisine. Owner and chef Hayrettin Gundogdu clearly marks the vegan dishes on a menu filled with many vegetarian options (he also makes note that the french fries are not vegetarian). The vegan white bean stew is thick and rich enough to be a meal on its own, particularly when served over rice ($6). Although tempting, it's better to opt for the small serving ($3) and save room for the stuffed vegetable plate ($9.50) or the sigara boregi combo ($9.25), a deep-fried sampler your arteries won't like but your taste buds will. Entrées are served with Turkish tea, and the unusual homemade bread is worth taking home an extra loaf for just $3. Anatolian Kabob is directly across the street from Lincoln Square's Davis Theatre (4614 North Lincoln Avenue), making it the perfect movie-and-dinner date spot.

**FULL MENU WITH MANY
VEGETARIAN OFFERINGS**

★ / $$
10. Andies

> 5253 North Clark Street
> Chicago, IL 60640
> 773.784.8616
> www.andiesres.com

LEBANESE AND GREEK

> *Hours:* Mon-Th 10:00 a.m. to 10:30 p.m.
> Fri-Sat 10:00 a.m. to 11:30 p.m.
> Sun 10:00 a.m. to 9:30 p.m.
> *Payment:* Credit cards accepted
> *Parking:* Small lot in back; after 6:00 p.m., free parking one block north at U.S. Bank
> *Alcohol:* Full bar
> *Atmosphere:* Midscale
>
> *Other locations:*
> 1467 West Montrose Avenue, Chicago, IL 60613
> 773.348.0654

Andies has blossomed from a diminutive storefront into a mod Mediterranean eatery. Andie and his family still run the show, and the earthy-yellow room still packs a crowd (especially on reduced-price martini Tuesdays), despite frequently slow service. Diners drool over the potato chop (mashed potato shells stuffed with vegetables and baked), pastichio (spinach, zucchini, carrots, and onions mixed with Greek pasta and baked), couscous (with sautéed peppers, onions, raisins, and almonds in a hot and spicy tomato sauce), and dolma, which is Andie's mom's recipe for stuffed grape leaves. Most dishes come with rice, either basmati or dill-infused. The menu offers many vegetarian items, but be sure to confirm when ordering. For example, the carrot puree soup is made with chicken stock. Entrées range from $10 to $14.

FULL MENU WITH MANY VEGETARIAN OFFERINGS

★ / $
11. Annapurna Fast Food

2608 West Devon Avenue
Chicago, IL 60659
773.764.1858

INDIAN

Hours:	Wed-Mon 11:00 a.m. to 9:00 p.m. Closed Tue
Payment:	Cash only
Parking:	Metered street parking, can be challenging on weekends
Alcohol:	No
Atmosphere:	Fast food, low-key

The good news is meal prices are the cheapest on Devon. The not-so-good news is that the ambiance is hot-dog-joint caliber. One word—plastics—describes everything from the aqua booths lining the narrow room to the cutlery to the dishware. It's best to know your bhindi (okra) from your malai kofta (fried cheese balls in creamy sauce) from channa masala (chickpeas), as items aren't described in English on the menu board and the order-takers behind the counter have thick accents. Masala dosas ($3.50) are a house favorite. The thali ($4.95) tops the price list and provides the menu mother lode: two vegetable dishes, dal, raita, rice pulao, two puri or chapati, papadum, pickles, and a dessert. Annapurna isn't haute cuisine, but it's good, filling food for minimal rupees.

VEGETARIAN WITH SOME VEGAN OFFERINGS

★ / $$
12. Arya Bhavan

2508 West Devon Avenue
Chicago, IL 60659
773.274.5800
www.aryabhavan.com

INDIAN

Hours:	Tue-Th 11:30 a.m. to 3:00 p.m., 5:00 p.m. to 10:00 p.m.
	Fri-Sat 11:30 a.m. to 3:00 p.m., 5:00 p.m. to 10:30 p.m.
	Sun 11:30 a.m. to 9:30 p.m.
	Closed Mon, except for major holidays
Payment:	Credit cards accepted
Parking:	Metered street parking, can be challenging on weekends, free parking after hours at Republic Bank on Devon at Washtenaw Street and Fairfield Avenue
Alcohol:	Beer and wine only
Atmosphere:	Casual

Arya Bhavan offers dishes from many of India's regions and ethnic groups. Try thalis ($12.99), which come in North Indian, South Indian, Gujarati, and Jain varieties. Sample the buffet, which is laden with varying items each day and is always accompanied by deliciously doughy naan. The buffet runs weekdays for lunch ($6.99), Friday for dinner ($9.99), and Saturday and Sunday all day ($9.99). A full menu is available, and most items can be made vegan upon request. Pav bhaji ($6.99), a sloppy joe–like, tomato-based concoction served on buns, is a specialty, as is lilwa ni kachori ($5.99), a fried dough ball stuffed with green peas. Kirti, the friendly owner, is happy to explain her creations and ingredients, and how she prepares 40,000 samosas each summer for the ten-day food festival, Taste of Chicago. Sadly, service wanes when she's not around. Dishes range from $7 to $10.

VEGETARIAN WITH SOME VEGAN OFFERINGS

★★ / $
13. Asiana

2546 North Clark Street
Chicago, IL 60614
773.296.9189

VIETNAMESE

Hours:	Tue-Sun 11:30 a.m. to 10:00 p.m. Closed Mon
Payment:	Credit cards accepted
Parking:	Street parking can be difficult
Alcohol:	BYO, no corkage fee
Atmosphere:	Casual, low-key spot

This small, plain space with exposed pipes and a smattering of Asian art seems more fitting for taking out than dining in. Regardless, the staff is attentive and the menu is balanced, with an impressive 16 strictly vegetarian dishes. Veggie options lean heavily on tofu and vegetables that are steamed, fried, or sautéed in Vietnamese sauces. Goi cuon chay ($3) are rolls of tofu and vegetables in a papery-thin wrap with a zippy side of plum sauce. Bun chay ($5.50) is a satisfying pick: a steaming bowl of rice noodles, tofu, and vegetables soaked in homemade sauce. Additionally, many of the regular entrées can be prepared with tofu. Tropical fruit drinks ($2.50), a nice complement to the spicy food, are freshly blended and served in a tall shake glass. Entrées from $4.25 to $8.95.

FULL MENU WITH MANY VEGETARIAN OPTIONS

★★ / $
14. Atomix

>1957 West Chicago Avenue
>Chicago IL 60622
>312.666.2649

MULTIETHNIC

Hours:	Mon-Fri 7:00 a.m. to 10:00 p.m.
	Sat-Sun 9:00 a.m. to 10:00 p.m.
Payment:	Cash only
Parking:	Metered street parking possible
Alcohol:	No
Atmosphere:	Coffee shop

Perhaps the quietest coffee shop on the planet, Atomix attracts the disheveled laptop and latte crowd: folks who want to be caffeinated and get some work done, but not at their own dining room table. On any given day Atomix can have just one person at each table, making a group or couple who wants to have a chat over lunch self-conscious about the noise. Cell phone users kindly step outside to busy Chicago Avenue to take their calls. But whether you are solo are not, Atomix is worth a stop for its veg-friendly sandwiches and other snacks. The cashier will give you a slick reusable menu on which you circle your order, adding broccoli and other ingredients to both hot and cold sandwiches ($5), which are delicious, if simple. Veggie chips are served with most dishes, and vegan burgers, salsas, a thick chili ($2.25), and vegan desserts round out the menu. A retro space-age theme permeates the painted interior.

**CAFE MENU WITH MANY
VEGETARIAN OFFERINGS**

★★★ / $$
15. bd's mongolian barbeque

3330 North Clark Street
Chicago, IL 60657
773.325.2300
www.bdsmongolianbarbeque.com

PAN-ASIAN

Hours:	Mon-Th 11:30 a.m. to 10:00 p.m.
	Fri-Sat 11:30 a.m. to 11:00 p.m.
	Sun noon to 10:00 p.m.
Payment:	Credit cards accepted
Parking:	Street parking can be difficult
Alcohol:	Full bar, with many specialty drinks
Atmosphere:	Midscale, DIY chain

Other locations:
See Collar Counties on page 161

With its kitsch and its T.G.I. Friday's–style drinks and dessert menu, it'd be easy to write this place off as yet another chain and go somewhere independent or more authentic. That would be a mistake. For $11.99 at lunch or $13.99 at dinner, you can help yourself to a series of all-you-can-eat trips to the barbeque, where you pile on your own stir-fry and sauces, and a chef cooks it on the grill, separating vegetarian bowls from those of meat eaters. (Vegans and those with allergies can request their meals be fried in a separate pan.) The ingredients line features many savory sauces, including an excellent black bean, with directions on the best ways to combine ingredients. When it comes to the meat area, a sign reads, "Vegetarians may advance to Step 2." Lower prices are available for one-trip servings and kid portions, and since everyone makes his or her own dish from fresh ingredients, there is no cause for complaints. To paraphrase Harry Caray, "Holy (no) cow!"

VEGETARIAN AND VEGAN OFFERINGS; MEAT, FISH, POULTRY, AND SEAFOOD ALSO SERVED

★★ / $
16. Bite Cafe

1039 North Western Avenue
Chicago, IL 60622
773.395.BITE (2483)

MULTIETHNIC

Hours:	*Mon-Th 11:00 a.m. to midnight*
	Fri 11:00 a.m. to 2:00 a.m.
	Sat-Sun 9:00 a.m. to 3:00 p.m. (brunch)
	Sat 6:00 p.m. to 2:00 a.m.
	Sun 6:00 p.m. to midnight
Payment:	*Credit cards accepted*
Parking:	*Street parking available*
Alcohol:	*BYO, no corkage fee*
Atmosphere:	*Hipster casual*

Next to the Empty Bottle nightclub, Bite Cafe attracts a twenty-something crowd before and after the live music shows. Bite's funky diner decor and large number of daily specials make it an inviting and affordable choice for a quick meal, even if you don't happen to already be in the neighborhood. Wise choices include the poblano quesadillas with ancho salsa ($4.50), a grilled eggplant sandwich ($5.50), and the Panzaella ($4.75), a Tuscan bread salad. Save room for one of the many daily desserts, especially if you see the chocolate pudding with sugar cookie combination listed on the chalkboard. The staff is friendlier than its Gen Y reputation and is exceedingly accommodating of dietary concerns.

CAFE MENU WITH MANY VEGETARIAN AND VEGAN OFFERINGS

★ / $
17. Cafe Ennui

6981 North Sheridan Road
Chicago, IL 60626
773.973.2233

AMERICAN

Hours:	Sun-Th 6:00 a.m. to 11:00 p.m.
	Fri-Sat 7:00 a.m. to midnight
Payment:	Cash only
Parking:	Street parking can be challenging
Alcohol:	None
Atmosphere:	Hip, college-hangout coffee shop

This eclectic coffee shop populated by Loyola students and Rogers Park residents draws strong opinions from patrons, both pro and con. But with its vegetarian-friendly menu and pleasant steps-from-the-lake location, it merits a mention. Coffee is the priority here, served strong and in lots of flavors and styles. For those who crave just a little something with their caffeine, Ennui offers a large array of baked goods, including muffins, cookies, and cakes, as well as focaccia and pizza bread for those seeking something savory. The kitchen also serves up a surprising array of sandwiches, soups, chili, and even pasta dishes, the bulk of which are vegetarian or vegan. The subterranean room can get a bit smoky at times, but in warmer weather, sitting outside in view of Lake Michigan, the atmosphere is pleasantly lazy.

MOSTLY VEGETARIAN

★★★ / $$
18. Caffe de Lucca

1721 North Damen Avenue
Chicago, IL 60647
773.342.6000

ITALIAN

Hours:	*Mon-Fri 6:00 a.m. to 11:00 p.m.*
	Sat-Sun 7:00 a.m. to 2:00 a.m.
Payment:	*Credit cards accepted*
Parking:	*Street parking can be challenging*
Alcohol:	*Full bar*
Atmosphere:	*European cafe*

Who knew that the heart of old-world Italy was smack in the middle of Wicker Park? The owners of Caffe de Lucca have cleverly designed a space that makes you feel like you are on holiday in a typical open-air plaza in Italy. A clothesline of laundry even hangs overhead. The food is equally appealing, with a wide selection of hot and cold panini sandwiches, all of which are beautifully presented. Also on the menu are remarkably large salads, soups, frittata, and other light breakfast, lunch, and dinner items. Most sandwiches come with salad, so there's no need to order one as an appetizer. Instead try the Cichetti, Venetian bar snacks that are Italy's answer to tapas, or sample the Bruschetta, which comes with four different spreads. Vegan brownies and organic chocolate cake round out the menu, but the desserts pale in comparison to the strong flavors of the savory dishes. Most dishes are priced between $7 and $12.

FULL MENU WITH MANY VEGETARIAN AND VEGAN OFFERINGS

★★ / $
19. Chicago Diner

3411 North Halsted Street
Chicago, IL 60657
773.935.6696

MULTIETHNIC

Hours:	Mon-Th 11:00 a.m. to 10:30 p.m.
	Fri 11:00 a.m. to 11:00 p.m.
	Sat 10:00 a.m. to 11:00 p.m.
	Sun 10:00 a.m. to 10:30 p.m.
Payment:	Credit cards accepted
Parking:	Street, free lot after 6:00 p.m. and on weekends
Alcohol:	Full bar

For the last twenty years, Chicago Diner has been the destination for vegetarian-only eating, plying hungry patrons with large portions of tofu omelets, tofu "fish" fillets, tofu loaf, and tofu everything else. Chicago Diner recipes are now in a cookbook, and its outstanding vegan desserts (mostly cakes) are also sold at Whole Foods and other stores throughout Chicago, which has only upped its profile. While the surrounding Lakeview neighborhood has become trendier and more fashionable over the last two decades, Chicago Diner has remained the same. That means the 1970s hippie vibe lives on, with a plain white-stucco interior, ponytailed male servers, and laid-back attitude. Some say the recent emphasis on seitan and tofu dishes pretending to be their meatier alternatives (such as a Reuben sandwich or sausage, biscuit, and gravy) misses the boat. But few restaurants offer so many options for vegetarians, vegans, and people with food allergies, and there's something to be said for consistency. The popular turkey-free Thanksgiving dinner is worth a try. Entrées $6 to $10.

VEGETARIAN WITH VEGAN OFFERINGS

★★ / $$
20. Cousin's

3038 West Irving Park Road
Chicago, IL 60618
773.478.6868
www.cousinschicago.com

Turkish/Mediterranean

Hours:	Mon-Th 11:30 a.m. to 10:00 p.m.
	Fri 11:30 a.m. to 11:00 p.m.
	Sat 10:00 a.m. to 11:00 p.m.
	Sun 10:00 a.m. to 10:00 p.m.
Payment:	Credit cards accepted
Parking:	Easy street parking
Alcohol:	Full bar
Atmosphere:	Cozy, with floor seating available

The humble storefront exterior belies the aphrodisiac delights inside. The red-toned room, candelabras, piped-in belly-dancing music, and dishes with dates, eggplant, and honey set romance sirens wailing. Appetizers like ezme (chopped tomato, onion, smoked red bell pepper, and walnuts, $6) and mujver (zucchini pancakes with scallions, Kasseri cheese, and herbs, $5) are tasty and beautifully presented. However, the entreés, like vegetarian mousakas (a three-inch-thick slice) and imam firinda (eggplant topped with bell peppers, onions, pine nuts, and feta in a garlic tomato sauce), are curiously bland. Nice touches include toasty pita bread and complimentary tea in traditional tulip-shaped glasses. The chocolate baklava ($2.50) wins raves for dessert. Entrées range from $10 to $15.

Full menu with many vegetarian offerings

★★ / $
21. Desert Rose Cafe

4410 North Kedzie Avenue
Chicago, IL 60625
773.866.2233

MIDDLE EASTERN

Hours:	Mon-Sun 10:00 a.m. to 2:00 a.m.
Payment:	Credit cards accepted
Parking:	Street parking
Alcohol:	BYO, no corkage fee
Atmosphere:	Quaint cafe with authentic Middle Eastern feel

Step into this bright pumpkin-and-gold-painted cafe and be transported to the Middle East. Mustachioed men jabber in Arabic on ever-present cell phones, while Arabic music drifts from the white latticed hutch. Smoking is prevalent in the twelve-table room, and, although there is a designated nonsmoking section, the air isn't exactly pure. Vegetarians can choose from a small but scrumptious selection of standards: creamy hummus, baba ghanooj, foul mudamas (fava beans), fattoush (toasted pita, tomato, and lettuce salad), and tabbouleh, each $3.95, as well as delicate, crunchy falafel (plate $5.95, sandwich $3.95). Inspired touches include a fiery green chili pepper sauce served atop the hummus and fava beans, and hot baked pita. Honey-drizzled desserts like baklava cap the meal and go well with coffee, served thick in tiny cups and spiced with cardamom. Or finish with a soothing yansoon (anise-flavored tea, $2.25).

**FULL MENU WITH MANY
VEGETARIAN OFFERINGS**

★★★ / $$
22. Dharma Garden Thai Cuisine

3109 West Irving Park Road
Chicago IL 60618
773.588.9140

Thai/Pan-Asian

Hours:	Tue-Th 11:00 a.m. to 9:30 p.m.
	Fri-Sat 11:00 a.m. to 10:00 p.m.
	Sun noon to 9:00 p.m.
Payment:	Credit cards accepted
Parking:	Metered street parking
Alcohol:	BYO, no corkage fee
Atmosphere:	Classier than typical Thai sit-down restaurant

Dharma Garden's emphasis is on health, and it's carried throughout the menu, through the restaurant's two rooms, and into the gift shop. The menu touts "wellness-filtered water," no MSG, and a reliance on brown rice, fruits, and vegetables. The staff's soothing demeanor and the room's melodic fountains contribute to the sense of wellness, and the food at Dharma does not sacrifice taste for health. Almost everything on the menu can be made with fresh tofu (not rubbery or packaged, as is often the case), seafood, or any number of imitation meats. The Mee Suao ("Long Life") noodles, with chives, mushrooms, ginger, and spinach are outstanding. Come with an open mind to try unexpected Asian dishes, and you won't be disappointed. Entrées are priced depending on the type of imitation meat or seafood included, and range from $6.95 to $11.95. Many appetizers and soups are less than $4.

Vegetarian and vegan offerings; fish also served

★★ / $$
23. Earwax Cafe

1561 North Milwaukee Avenue
Chicago, IL 60622
773.772.4019
www.earwaxcafe.com

AMERICAN

Hours:	Daily 8:00 a.m. to 11:00 p.m.
Payment:	Credit cards accepted
Parking:	Limited street parking, especially on evenings and weekends
Alcohol:	No
Atmosphere:	Funky circus diner

Tapestries hawking circus acts like Ostrich Boy and the King of Blades and Whips hang from the orange, blue, and green walls at Earwax Cafe. Booths at the front of the restaurant call to mind seats from a carousel. But the food and the laid-back attitude are what attract the grunge, Goth, artist, musician mélange of Wicker Park. The Veggie Black Bean Burger ($6.95) is a neighborhood staple that tastes even better in its Messy version ($7.25) topped with caramelized onions, coleslaw, cheddar, and chipotle barbecue sauce. The goat cheese quesadilla ($7.75) with roasted red peppers, corn, jalapenos, and cilantro pesto tastes so good you almost don't want to swallow it. Plus there's a full breakfast menu, vegan desserts, a back patio for outdoor dining during nice weather, and a video rental store downstairs.

**VEGETARIAN OFFERINGS;
SOME MEAT SANDWICHES ALSO SERVED**

★★★ / $$
24. El Tinajon

2054 West Roscoe Street
Chicago, IL 60618
773.525.8455

GUATEMALAN

Hours:	Mon, Wed-Th 11:00 a.m. to 8:00 p.m.
	Fri-Sat 11:00 a.m. to 9:00 p.m.
	Closed Sun, Tue
Payment:	Credit cards accepted
Parking:	Street parking possible
Alcohol:	Full bar
Atmosphere:	Cozy casual

The small El Tinajon was a staple in Roscoe Village long before the neighborhood became a magnet for high-end and trendy restaurants. Despite the influx of surrounding eateries, El Tinajon still holds its own (and commands a wait for tables). Its ample menu is filled with Guatemalan specialties—dishes that are similar enough to Mexican food not to be intimidating, but unusual enough to be exciting. The Combo Vegetariano ($9.75), with a shepe tamal (platano leaf and black bean), potato taco, and a Guatemalan enchilada, is perhaps the best bet for first-timers. The Plato San Lucas ($9.25) is an appealing dish of green beans, squash seeds, and chipotle pepper sauce. Desserts are equally unusual, including plantain dough with sweet beans ($1) or in sweet chocolate spice mole sauce ($2.25).

**FULL MENU WITH SOME
VEGETARIAN OFFERINGS**

★★ / $
25. The Emerald City

2852 North Clark Street
Chicago, IL 60657
773.477.0555

MIDDLE EASTERN

Hours:	Mon-Sat 10:00 a.m. to 10:30 p.m.
	Sun 10:00 a.m. to 8:30 p.m.
Payment:	Credit cards accepted
Parking:	Street parking can be difficult
Alcohol:	No
Atmosphere:	Simple cafe with counter salad bar

Follow the Yellow Brick Road to this small, no-frills cafe with deli-style tables and counter, ideal for a quick bite or solo dining. The menu focuses on healthy Middle Eastern fare. With a salad bar ($3.99 a pound) that takes center stage, Emerald City aims to be lighter than your standard gyros joint. Beyond lettuce and tomatoes, the hot and cold bar ($3.99 a pound) features steamed vegetables, curried rice, vegetarian lasagna, and more. A full menu featuring veggie burgers, a selection of vegetable soups, crispy falafel, spinach pie, grape leaves, and hummus means there's no shortage of protein-packed vegetarian options. For something sweet, try fruit smoothies (made dairy or non and available with added protein), fresh-squeezed juices, or frozen yogurt (also available in nondairy). Items range from $2.29 to $4.99.

FULL MENU WITH MANY VEGETARIAN OPTIONS

★★★ / $$
26. Ethio Cafe

3462 North Clark Street
Chicago, IL 60657
773.929.8300

ETHIOPIAN

Hours:	*Tue-Fri 5:00 to 11:00 p.m.*
	Sat-Sun 1:00 p.m. to 11:00 p.m.
	Closed Mon
Payment:	*Credit cards accepted*
Parking:	*Street parking can be difficult, especially during Cubs games*
Alcohol:	*Full bar*
Atmosphere:	*Casual restaurant with live music*

With its funky music and traditional folk art, this spacious dining room has enough regional flavor to transport you far from the Windy City. The exotic food and aromas complete your delightful trip. Start with a fruit shake or a carafe of tej (Ethiopian honey wine, $10.95) and an order of lentil salad or vegetarian sambussa (veggie-filled pastry). Vegetarian main courses, which mix lentils, chickpeas, and other vegetables with garlic, ginger, and red pepper sauce, are all dairy-free and surprisingly filling. The vegetarian buffet, offered Saturdays and Sundays from 1:00 to 9:00 p.m., is a spread of soups, salads, and stews for just $7.95. Service is friendly, but busy weekends suffer from an over-extended staff. Entrées range from $6.95 to $12.95

FULL MENU WITH MANY VEGETARIAN AND VEGAN OPTIONS

★★ / $$
27. Flat Top Grill

319 West North Avenue
Chicago, IL 60610
312.787.7676

PAN-ASIAN

Hours:	Sun-Th 11:30 a.m. to 10:00 p.m.
	Fri-Sat 11:30 a.m. to 11:00 p.m.
Payment:	Credit cards accepted
Parking:	Nearby pay lot, valet available after 5:00 p.m., street parking difficult
Alcohol:	Full bar
Atmosphere:	Midscale, DIY chain

Other locations:
3200 North Southport Avenue, Chicago, IL 60657
773.665.8100
See also Downtown on page 89; Suburban Cook County on page 143

This make-your-own stir-fry chain is a great place to take the whole brood. Grab a bowl from the stir-fry bar and fill it with your choice of rice, noodles, and fresh vegetables, then top it off with a few ladles from the selection of sauces (meat and fish eaters can also fill a side dish with beef, chicken, or seafood). Add a color-coded stick to turn your stir-fry into a wrap or soup, have it piled atop a bed of greens, or request it be cooked in a separate wok to avoid cross-contamination. The selection of ingredients changes quarterly to reflect local growing seasons. There's also a small menu of Asian-inspired appetizers, plus martinis and fruity tropical drinks. Unlimited trips to the stir-fry bar cost $7.99 at lunch and $12.99 at dinner for adults; meals for children ten and under are $4.99.

VEGETARIAN AND VEGAN OFFERINGS; MEAT, FISH, POULTRY, AND SEAFOOD ALSO SERVED

★★ / $$
28. Flying Saucer

1123 North California Avenue
Chicago, IL 60622
773.342.9076

MULTIETHNIC

Hours:	Tue-Fri 7:00 a.m. to 10:00 p.m.
	Sat 8:00 a.m. to 10:00 p.m.
	Sun 8:00 a.m. to 3:00 p.m.
	Closed Mon
Payment:	Credit cards accepted
Parking:	Ample street parking
Alcohol:	BYO, no corkage fee
Atmosphere:	Classic diner

This Humboldt Park favorite looks like the diner of your youth. But the emphasis on local ingredients and healthy options, not to mention veg-friendly, makes it oh so twenty-first century. Breakfast is served until 3:00 p.m., so you have your choice of dishes such as sweet potato and tofu hash ($6.95), the Flying Tofu Bowl ($7.75), and the warm lentil and beet salad ($7.50) almost any time of day. The homemade veggie burger ($6.75) sounds tempting after one too many Boca Burgers, but can be mushy and bland. The staff is friendly and accommodating to diners with kids. Feel free to bring vegetarian little ones and encourage them to try the pasta of the week or the pierogies ($5.75). If that won't fly, there's an impressive grilled cheese ($5.50) or cheese quesadillas ($5.75).

FULL MENU WITH MANY VEGETARIAN AND VEGAN OPTIONS

★★ / $
29. Fresh Choice

3351 North Broadway Avenue
Chicago, IL 60657
773.248.5000

MULTIETHNIC

Hours:	Sun-Th 10:00 a.m. to 10:00 p.m.
	Fri-Sat 10:00 a.m. to 11:00 p.m.
Payment:	Cash only
Parking:	Metered street parking
Alcohol:	No
Atmosphere:	Take-out spot with juice bar

Other locations:
See Downtown on page 92

Who knew comfort food could be so good for you? With a menu that includes beverages that allow you to add nutritious "hits"—from brewer's yeast to bee pollen—this Old Town storefront shop accomplishes it. The menu boasts healthy options, including soups, subs, salads, and baked potatoes with a variety of toppings, all in the $2.50 to $6.75 range. The veggie sub ($5.45), with vegetables and three cheeses on warm crusty bread, is as filling as its meaty counterparts. Fresh Choice's true claims to fame are its smoothies, which are made with either skim milk or fresh fruit juice, and are tasty, albeit pricey ($3.42). The cozy decor is that of a local hangout, with counter service, white boards serving as menus, and a bulletin board with Polaroids of customers' babies (all holding smoothies). Bright yellow walls, contrasting with the whir of a blender, complete the picture.

FULL MENU WITH MANY VEGETARIAN OPTIONS

★★★ / $$
30. Handlebar Bar and Grill

2311 West North Avenue
Chicago, IL 60647
773.384.9546
www.handlebarchicago.com

MULTIETHNIC

Hours:	Mon-Fri 4:00 p.m. to 11:00 p.m.
	Sat-Sun 1:00 p.m. to 1:00 a.m.
Payment:	Credit cards accepted
Parking:	Ample street parking
Alcohol:	Full bar with daily beer specials
Atmosphere:	Neighborhood bar with live music

Even if you haven't ridden a bike since you called it a "two-wheeler," you'll enjoy the bike-vibe at Handlebar. From the old bicycle art on the walls to the Monday discounts for bike messengers, spokes are taken seriously here. But the theme doesn't overshadow a diverse vegetarian and vegan-friendly menu. A yin-yang symbol next to menu items indicates whether or not a dish can be made vegan. The West African Ground Nut Stew ($7), with sweet potato, coconut, zucchini, and kale, is an unusual offering. The wasabi baked tofu ($8) and the Green Meanie sandwich ($7 for avocado, feta-herb spread, spinach, and sprouts) are also interesting twists. But Handlebar serves up classics, too, such as barbeque seitan sandwiches ($8) and vegetable lasagna ($9). The exposed brick walls and impressive bar are the perfect accent for late night live music that fills Handlebar's rooms.

FULL MENU WITH MANY VEGETARIAN AND VEGAN OFFERINGS

★★ / $
31. Hashalom

2905 West Devon Avenue
Chicago, IL 60659
773.465.5675

ISRAELI/MOROCCAN

Hours:	Mon-Fri noon to 9:00 p.m. Closed Sat-Sun
Payment:	Cash and checks only
Parking:	Metered street parking
Alcohol:	BYO, no corkage fee
Atmosphere:	Ethnic-flavored family diner

Hashalom, at the western edge of Devon Avenue's international food corridor, serves a mix of cuisines that makes it fairly unique. People ranging in age from toddler to senior and every decade in between eat at simple tables under walls festooned with latch hook "Israel" rugs, copper pots, and images of rabbis. The Israeli combo ($8) offers generous portions of Jerusalem salad, hummus, baba ghanooj, eggplant, and crispy falafel. The Moroccan combo ($8) has matbukha (cooked, seasoned tomatoes), eggplant, beets, carrot salad, and atomically spiced peppers. Bourekas (phyllo triangles filled with melted feta and sautéed onions, $4.25) and shakshouka (two eggs sunny side up, splashed across cooked tomatoes, onions, and peppers, $4) are other palate pleasers. Vegetarian couscous ($9) is available Friday nights only. Entrées range from $4 to $10.

FULL MENU WITH MANY VEGETARIAN OFFERINGS

★★ / $$
32. Heartland Cafe

> 7000 North Glenwood Avenue
> Chicago, IL 60626
> 773.465.8005
> www.heartlandcafe.com

AMERICAN

Hours:	Mon-Th 7:00 a.m. to 10:00 p.m.
	Fri 7:00 a.m. to 11:00 p.m.
	Sat 8:00 a.m. to 11:00 p.m.
	Sun 8:00 a.m. to 10:00 p.m.
Payment:	Credit cards accepted
Parking:	Street parking possible
Alcohol:	Full bar
Atmosphere:	Eclectic, family-friendly, earth-friendly restaurant and bar

Since 1976, the Heartland has served as part restaurant, part bar, part performance space, and part community center for eclectic and bohemian East Rogers Park residents. At breakfast on a Saturday morning, you might see the Alderman holding a political meeting. Weeknights you might be dining to the background of a poetry jam. The menu offers a wide array of choices. At breakfast, in addition to the nearly twenty egg and omelet choices, Heartland serves up vegan dishes such as scrambled tofu, and granola with fruit. But it's at lunch and dinner that the vegan diner will truly feel at home with such choices as the macro plate (brown rice, beans, steamed greens, and mushroom gravy), the "big heart" lentil burger, and the barbeque seitan. Burritos, chili, daily-changing soups, salads, and sides like sweet potato fries round out the menu. One note of caution: with frequent open mikes and other events, the restaurant is not always conducive to quiet conversation. Call ahead or check the Web site to see what's on the calendar.

**FULL MENU WITH MANY
VEGETARIAN OFFERINGS**

★★★ / $$
33. Hema's Kitchen

6406 North Oakley Avenue
Chicago, IL 60645
773.338.1627

INDIAN/PAKISTANI

Hours:	Daily noon to 9:30 p.m.
Payment:	Credit cards accepted
Parking:	Street parking, can be challenging on weekend nights
Alcohol:	BYO, no corkage fee
Atmosphere:	No-frills, casual eatery

Other locations:
Hema's Kitchen II, 2411 North Clark Street
 Chicago, IL 60614, 773.529.1705

There is no shortage of vegetarian- and vegetarian-friendly Indian restaurants in Chicago, particularly in the Devon Avenue area. But Chef Hema Potla makes all the meals herself at her hybrid Indian and Pakistani restaurant, and the results are more intensely flavorful and more properly spiced than many of the area's eateries. The dal makhni (lentils with onions, tomatoes, ginger, and spices) isn't overly starchy as it can be, and even the deep-fried vegetable pakoras ($2.75) somehow aren't too greasy. Hema's Kitchen expanded to the adjoining storefront, reflecting how popular this mom-and-pop stop is. But even that wasn't enough to accommodate crowds, so a second location opened on Clark Street in Lincoln Park. Because Hema makes everything herself, expect service to be slow. Entrées typically under $10.

FULL MENU WITH MANY VEGETARIAN OFFERINGS

★★ / $
34. Jal Hind

2658 West Devon Avenue
Chicago, IL 60659
773.973.3400

INDIAN

Hours:	Wed-Mon 10:00 a.m. to 8:00 p.m. Closed Tue
Payment:	Cash only
Parking:	Metered street parking, can be challenging on weekends
Alcohol:	No
Atmosphere:	Cafeteria style

A familiarity with Indian cuisine and knowing some Hindi will certainly enhance the ordering experience at Jal Hind, a storefront Indian restaurant in the heart of Chicago's Indian restaurant row. Order from a menu board over ancient refrigerator cases that hold an array of Indian sweets like jalebi ($3) and gulab jamun ($4.50). Stainless-steel warming trays hold the savories, but the naan is baked to order. A stack of buttery naan and Styrofoam cup of chana masala that is burn-your-lips spicy runs about $3.50 and is just the right size to qualify as a hearty lunch. Jal Hind is not an inviting place to sit and eat (although there are tables), but for good, authentic vegetarian Indian takeout at extremely reasonable prices, it fits the bill.

VEGETARIAN

★ / $$$
35. Jane's

1655 West Cortland Street
Chicago, IL 60622
773.862.JANE (5263)
www.janesrestaurant.com

AMERICAN CONTEMPORARY

Hours:	Mon-Th 5:00 p.m. to 10:00 p.m.
	Fri 5:00 p.m. to 11:00 p.m.
	Sat 11:00 a.m. to 11:00 p.m.
	Sun 11:00 a.m. to 10:00 p.m.
Payment:	Credit cards accepted
Parking:	Street parking can be difficult weekends
Alcohol:	Full bar, $15 corkage fee for BYO
Atmosphere:	Upscale hip bistro

This small Bucktown restaurant has a reputation for being more veg-friendly than it is, perhaps because of its emphasis on seasonal produce and locally grown ingredients. That said, there are always more than a few solid vegetarian options on the menu at Jane's, a menu that changes with the seasons. The winter corn chowder is fine, if bland, but the salads, such as one with corn and dried cherries mixed with the greens, are inventive and fresh. Popular veg-friendly entrées include a goat cheese and tofu burrito and several spicy pasta dishes. There is typically one vegan item on the menu; entrée prices range from $12.95 to $23.95. In some ways, Jane's success has also been its downfall. Eager to let in a waiting crowd, the staff often discourages diners from having a leisurely meal. The crowd at the bar, where smoking is permitted, tends to be young, lively, and fun.

FULL MENU WITH SOME VEGETARIAN OFFERINGS

★★ / $
36. Jim's Grill

1429 West Irving Park Road
Chicago, IL 60613
773.525.4050

KOREAN

Hours:	*Mon-Fri 8:30 a.m. to 3:30 p.m.*
	Sat 9:00 a.m. to 3:00 p.m.
Payment:	*Cash only*
Parking:	*Street parking possible*
Alcohol:	*No*
Atmosphere:	*No-frills luncheonette*

Owned by the vegan gurus behind Amitabul (see page 20 for details), Jim's Grill is a beat-up lunch counter, with crumbling ceiling tiles and once-bright decor. But people don't come to Jim's for the ambiance. They come for a selection of bargain-priced vegan and vegetarian Korean specialties, as well as breakfasts that fit the restaurant's vibe. Favorites include kim chee pancakes ($5.95), hot spicy wheat noodles ($5.50), and the vegetable maki roll ($2.95). Bi bim bop can be ordered with or without egg. Morning meal options include a spicy Korean-style omelette ($3.50) and egg-white omelettes. Service is fast, but don't feel that you need to hurry out. Best to have an extra cup of ginseng tea and join in the lively political discourse at the counter.

FULL MENU WITH MANY VEGETARIAN AND VEGAN OFFERINGS

★★ / $
37. Jinx Cafe

1928 West Division Street
Chicago, IL 60622
773.645.3667

AMERICAN COFFEE SHOP

Hours:	*Mon-Fri 7:00 a.m. to 11:00 p.m.*
	Sat 9:00 a.m. to 8:00 p.m.
	Sun 9:00 a.m. to 11:00 p.m.
Payment:	*Cash only*
Parking:	*Street parking possible, but difficult on weekend nights*
Alcohol:	*BYO, no corkage fee*
Atmosphere:	*Alternative-rock college coffee shop*

Those over the age of twenty-five may feel out of their element at Jinx, with its red-and-black decor, blaring music, and plethora of band posters. At first glance this is a mere coffee shop with a crowd of discontents sipping Joe in booths, at tables, or at the counter. But just like the light fixtures made from coffee cans, there's some ingenuity at work at Jinx. The grilled sandwiches beat those served at better-known chains by a long shot. Try the Benny, made with cheese and "every single veggie we have," served on marble rye ($5). The hummus plate, veggie chili, and Jinx salad are all great options, and it's hard to spend even $10 total. A cherry Coke here is the real thing, mixed with syrup, not served from a can. Just don't come seeking peace and quiet.

FULL MENU WITH MANY VEGETARIAN OPTIONS

★★ / $$
38. John's Place

1200 West Webster Street
Chicago, IL 60614
773.525.6670

MULTIETHNIC

Hours:	*Tue-Th 11:00 a.m. to 10:00 p.m.*
	Fri 11:00 a.m. to 11:00 p.m.
	Sat 8:00 a.m. to 11:00 p.m.
	Sun 8:00 a.m. to 9:00 p.m.
	Closed Mon
Payment:	*Credit cards accepted*
Parking:	*Street parking*
Alcohol:	*Full bar*
Atmosphere:	*Family-friendly by day, couples-friendly by night*

This cozy two-room favorite delivers more than expected. With a bar, fireplace, votive-topped tables, and meat on the menu, it has the feel of a casual neighborhood grill—but it also has plenty of vegetarian options, making it an ideal spot for mixed groups of vegetarians and non. The service is decent, and the food is above average. Most of the appetizers, including portobello pot stickers ($5.95) and cheese quesadillas ($6.95), and all the sides ($2.50), such as mashed sweet potatoes and Chinese noodles, are vegetarian. The veggie burrito, chock-full of veggies, smothered with cheese, and served with brown rice and mixed greens, is tasty and filling. Other vegetarian-friendly entrées ($5.95 to $9.50) include meal-sized salads, grilled tofu, and vegetable kabobs with a kick. On Tuesdays and Thursdays, take advantage of half-priced bottles of wine.

FULL MENU WITH MANY VEGETARIAN OPTIONS

★★ / $$
39. Kabul House

   1629 North Halsted Street
   Chicago, IL 60614
   312.751.1029

   AFGHAN

Hours:	Tue-Th 4:00 p.m. to 10:30 p.m.
	Fri-Sat 4:00 p.m. to 11:00 p.m.
	Closed Mon
Payment:	Credit cards accepted
Parking:	Street parking challenging
Alcohol:	BYO, no corkage fee
Atmosphere:	Cozy casual

   Other locations:
   See Suburban Cook County on page 147

This basement-level restaurant is a Middle Eastern oasis across the street from the Steppenwolf Theatre, along a strip where decent cheap eats are increasingly rare. Kabul House's Afghan take on Middle Eastern favorites results in a sweeter hybrid of Persian and Indian delights. The must-try entrée is the kadu chalau ($8.95), a sautéed pumpkin dish with yogurt and mint. Another strong contender is the sabzi chalau ($8.95), sautéed spinach over basmati rice. Several of the rice dishes come with carrots and raisins to sweeten the pot. An appetizer of dal ($4.25) brings the flavors of India's seasoned lentils. Pita bread arrives thicker than standard, and is replenished by an attentive wait staff.

FULL MENU WITH MANY VEGETARIAN OFFERINGS

★★ / $$$
40. Karyn's Bistro

1901 North Halsted Street
Chicago, IL 60614
312.255.1590

RAW FOOD

Hours:	Daily 11:30 a.m. to 10:00 p.m.
Payment:	Credit cards accepted
Parking:	Street parking possible
Alcohol:	BYO, $5 corkage fee
Atmosphere:	Upscale serene bistro, adjacent take-out cafe

Giant square glass plates bring a plethora of raw food concoctions to a white-cloth-covered table. On the plate may be deep-dish pizza ($11), polenta with shiitake mushrooms ($14), or a Sun Burger on herbed raw bread ($12). All of the dishes are whipped up by Karyn Calabrese in Karyn's kitchen. Notice the lack of the word cooked: Everything at Karyn's Bistro and her adjacent cafe is raw, organic, and vegan (some dishes do contain honey). Raw foods are not for everyone. From the texture to the saltiness, they do not always closely resemble the dishes they are purported to be. Such qualities don't make them inferior, just different. Open yourself up to the serenity of Karyn's lifestyle (natural life products and treatments like colonics are also available on-site) and try a few raw dishes without comparing them to their cooked varieties. Perfect for those nights that are too hot to turn on the stove.

VEGAN RAW FOODS, SOME HONEY USED

★★★ / $$
41. Katerina's

1920 West Irving Park Road
Chicago, IL 60613
773.348.7592
www.katerinas.com

MEDITERRANEAN

Hours:	Mon 4:00 p.m. to 2:00 a.m.
	Tue-Sat 11:00 a.m. to 2:00 a.m.
	Sun 11:00 a.m. to midnight
Payment:	Credit cards accepted
Parking:	Limited street parking
Alcohol:	Full bar
Atmosphere:	Neighborhood jazz bar

Katerina's is a classy, yet comfortable, neighborhood watering hole where owner Katerina Carson will treat you like family. The menu is not extensive, but the selections that are there are sure to please, especially the wealth of vegetarian appetizers. Roasted red peppers ($8) are filled with asiago cheese and sprinkled with balsamic vinegar. The oven-roasted ambrosia ($9)—red peppers, zucchini, and yellow squash marinated in a balsamic-dijon dressing, served on French bread, and topped with melted cheese and capers—is a meal-sized bruschetta minus the tomatoes. Tiropitákita (phyllo filled with ricotta, feta, and goat cheese served with Amaretto-cinnamon oranges) comes in plate ($7) or platter ($13) size. And you can always make your own panini (price varies with ingredients). Saturday and Sunday brunch features oven-baked skillet omelets ($7 to $9) and homemade Greek yogurt with caramelized figs and walnuts ($6). There is a $5 cover most nights.

FULL MENU WITH MANY VEGETARIAN OFFERINGS

★★ / $
42. Kopi: A Traveler's Cafe

5317 North Clark Street
Chicago, IL 60640
773.989.5674

MULTIETHNIC

Hours:	*Mon-Th 8:00 a.m. to 11:00 p.m.*
	Fri 8:00 a.m. to midnight
	Sat 9:00 a.m. to midnight
	Sun 10:00 a.m. to 11:00 p.m.
Payment:	*Credit cards accepted*
Parking:	*Street parking, can be difficult on weekend nights*
Alcohol:	*No*
Atmosphere:	*Relaxing, smoke-free coffee shop*

Taking its name from the Indonesian word for coffee, this cozy, smoke-free Andersonville cafe and travel bookshop offers a relaxed atmosphere and vegetarian-friendly menu that satisfies for a snack or a full meal. True to its coffee shop heritage, Kopi's expansive menu has an array of hot drinks, including multiple styles of coffee; black, green, and medicinal teas; and hot chocolate. On the cooler side, Kopi offers smoothies of the day, organic juices, and sodas. For the most part, Kopi steers away from faux meat products (although many people swear by the "tofurky" sandwiches and tempeh burgers). Instead, the emphasis is on freshly prepared offerings like the Libido Burrito (a roasted red pepper and goat cheese sandwich) and the simple but tasty Balkan (Swiss cheese, lettuce, onion, and tomato on black bread). Cheese can be omitted from any item. For dessert, choose from cakes, cookies, and other goodies (mostly not vegan). Breakfast, served all day, includes light muffin and bagel fare, egg dishes, and French toast, served only weekends. Main dishes run about $5 to $10.

VEGETARIAN; EGGS AND FISH ALSO SERVED

★★ / $$
43. Leona's

3877 North Elston Avenue
Chicago, IL 60618
773.267.7287
www.leonas.com

ITALIAN

Hours:	Mon-Th 11:30 a.m. to 10:30 p.m.
	Fri 11:30 a.m. to 11:30 p.m.
	Sat noon to 11:30 p.m.
	Sun noon to 10:00 p.m.
Payment:	Credit cards accepted
Parking:	Free lot
Alcohol:	Full bar, including organic beer and wine
Atmosphere:	Family-friendly midscale

Other locations in North Side Chicago:
3215 North Sheffield Avenue, 773.327.8861
6935 North Sheridan Road, 773.764.5757
1936 West Augusta Boulevard, 773.292.4300
7443 West Irving Park Road, 773.625.3636
See also Downtown on page 99; South Side on page 125; Suburban Cook County on page 149

Leona's bills itself as a "closet vegetarian" joint with an emphasis on fresh, wholesome ingredients. In other words, no "frankenfoods." So dig in reassuringly to the portobello and white mushrooms in whole wheat ravioli; vegan burger made of tofu, sliced mushrooms, sunflower seeds, and rolled oats; and grilled flatbread wraps stuffed with tofu, roasted veggies, or hummus. The deep-dish pizza ($21.50 for a large) reigns supreme, made with a touch of cornmeal in the crust. Imaginative toppings include pesto or hummus instead of typical tomato sauce. Soy cheese is also available. Entrées range from $11 to $25 and pasta/sandwiches/burgers from $8.50 to $13. Leona's has eighteen locations throughout the city and suburbs.

FULL MENU WITH MANY VEGETARIAN AND VEGAN OFFERINGS

★ / $
44. Letizia's Natural Bakery

2144 West Division Street
Chicago, IL 60622
773.342.1011

MULTIETHNIC

Hours:	Mon-Fri 6:00 a.m. to 11:00 p.m.
	Sat-Sun 6:30 a.m. to 11:00 p.m.
Payment:	Credit cards accepted for purchases more than $10
Parking:	Metered street parking possible
Alcohol:	No
Atmosphere:	Natural bakery and coffee shop

This all-natural bakery has become a Wicker Park destination, not just for those who want a muffin to go. With its wireless Internet access and laid-back vibe, Letizia's is a local hangout with more than decent eats. The veg-friendly sandwich menu wins raves. Favorites include The Grazer ($5.50), with spinach, mushrooms, red onions, tomato, cheese, and balsamic vinaigrette on focaccia, and Fabio's SPIN ($4), which is the vegan version of the same sandwich. Daily soup specials start at $2.50, and pizzas start at $12. Salads and pasta dishes include the Pasta Broccolino ($3.25 small or $5.50 large), with broccoli, olive oil, and roasted garlic. Everything in the store is made without bleached flours, hydrogenated oils, or preservatives. Fresh fruit cups ($3.50) are available with seasonal fruit, but for most sweet tooths, the lure of the daily baked desserts will be strong.

CAFE MENU WITH MANY VEGETARIAN AND VEGAN OFFERINGS

★★ / $$$
45. Lovitt

>1466 North Ashland Avenue
>Chicago, IL 60622
>773.252.1466
>
>**AMERICAN**
>
>| | |
>|---|---|
>| Hours: | Wed-Sat 6:00 p.m. to 10:00 p.m. |
>| | Sun 10:00 a.m. to 3:00 p.m. (brunch) |
>| | Sun 5:00 p.m. to 9:00 p.m. (dinner) |
>| Payment: | Credit cards accepted |
>| Parking: | Street parking possible |
>| Alcohol: | BYO, no corkage fee |
>| Atmosphere: | Intimate date spot |

The size of a studio apartment, Lovitt is a creative haven of cuisine made with organic and locally grown produce, with an emphasis on seasonal dishes. The menu changes daily as a result. Each night the menu typically offers five to seven entrées. Recent vegetarian choices have included a pot pie, a hearty lasagna with beet noodles, and pasta primavera with tofu and soy milk sauce. Cheese plates, vegan lentil soup, and vegan lemon and asparagus puree are typically of the lighter fare. Because the menu is so pliable, some days are more veg-friendly than others, and, of course, some dishes are more flavorful than others. Expect artful presentations and prices (starting at $13) to match. Sunday brunch is an area favorite. Despite having only ten tables, the combination of 1980s and 1990s music and high ceilings makes Lovitt loud.

FULL MENU WITH VEGETARIAN AND VEGAN OFFERINGS

★★★ / $$
46. Lula Cafe

2537 North Kedzie Boulevard
Chicago, IL 60647
773.489.9554
www.lulacafe.com

MULTIETHNIC

Hours:	Sun-Mon, Wed-Th 9:00 a.m. to 10:00 p.m.
	Fri-Sat 9:00 a.m. to 11:00 p.m.
	Closed Tue
Payment:	Credit cards accepted
Parking:	Metered street parking
Alcohol:	Full bar
Atmosphere:	Arty casual

Using local and organic ingredients, Lula is one of the few restaurants in Chicago where nonvegetarians, vegetarians, and even vegans leave equally impressed and satisfied. Great starters include chilled peanut satay noodles with spinach and marinated tofu, a spicy shiitake mushroom quesadilla, and beet bruschetta served with arugula, goat cheese, and a garlic vinaigrette ($5.50 to $7.50). Popular entrées include a Moroccan chickpea and sweet potato tagine, the spicy peanut butter tineka sandwich with sweet soy sauce, and the garlicky Pasta Yiayia, featuring bucatini with cinnamon, brown butter, and feta cheese ($5.50 to $8). Special appetizers and entrées change frequently to highlight seasonal produce, and tend to be a little more expensive than regular menu items ($11 to $23). The kitchen can usually make options vegan on request. Like specials, desserts also rotate in and out but usually include a selection of sorbets and ice creams, classics like organic carrot cake, and slightly more daring options like a bittersweet chocolate tart with grilled dates and a balsamic gastrique ($6 to $7).

FULL MENU WITH MANY VEGETARIAN OPTIONS

★★ / $$
47. M. Henry

5707 North Clark Street
Chicago, IL 60660
773.561.1600

CONTINENTAL BREAKFAST, BRUNCH AND LUNCH

Hours:	Tue-Fri 7:00 a.m. to 2:30 p.m.
	Sat-Sun 8:00 a.m. to 3:00 p.m.
	Closed Mon
Payment:	Credit cards accepted
Parking:	Street parking fairly easy
Alcohol:	BYO, no corkage fee
Atmosphere:	Bright, minimalist cafe

On the northern edge of Andersonville, M. Henry is one of the area's most welcoming brunch and lunch spots. The light, airy room is decorated with old window frames hung from the ceiling, giving tables a little sense of privacy without making the room dark or the floor plan unwieldy. The menu is similarly clever, with vegan and vegetarian options at both breakfast and lunch. M. Henry is one of the few places in the city to serve yuba, which is made from the cream that rises to the top of hot soymilk when tofu is made. Yuba is found in the breakfast Vegan Epiphany ($6.50) with house potatoes, red and green peppers, and organic tofu. Other hits are the veggie Dagwood sandwich ($6.95) that, just like the cartoon version suggests, is too big to get your mouth around all at once. Red onion, miso glaze, avocado, and other layers are stacked between multigrain bread—topped with an olive, of course. The Simply Hotcakes ($7.95) are served with a pomegranate syrup, and the pepper and egg sandwich ($5.95) is an ample meal on its own. Everything is made to order, and M. Henry is popular, so don't expect fast-food turnaround times.

FULL MENU WITH MANY VEGETARIAN AND SOME VEGAN OPTIONS

★★ / $$
48. Mama Desta's Red Sea Restaurant

3216 North Clark Street
Chicago, IL 60657
773.935.7561

ETHIOPIAN

Hours:	Wed-Mon 4:00 p.m. to 11:00 p.m. Closed Tue
Payment:	Credit cards accepted
Parking:	Street parking can be difficult
Alcohol:	Full bar
Atmosphere:	Modest, cheerful restaurant

With dishes chock-full of legumes, vegetables, and exotic spices, this unpretentious restaurant serves up traditional Ethiopian cuisine ideal for vegetarians looking for a new flavor. Soft music plays in the modest salmon-pink-and-green dining room and adjacent bar. A small but friendly staff happily explains the cuisine, which features savory stew-like combinations of vegetables (and/or meat) called wats and alitchas (ranging from $7.40 to $10.25). The dishes, including yesmir wat (pureed lentils) and d'nitch (potatoes, carrots, and broccoli), are served with injera, the spongy unleavened bread used instead of utensils to scoop up mouthfuls. Yestom kilkil, a combination of four vegetarian dishes, is a good option, but no matter what you choose, this food is meant for sharing—especially while enjoying a glass of traditional tej, the sweet orange-colored honey wine.

FULL MENU WITH MANY VEGETARIAN OPTIONS

★★ / $$
49. Moti Mahal

1035 West Belmont Avenue
Chicago, IL 60657
773.348.4392

INDIAN

Hours:	*Sun-Th noon to 9:30 p.m.*
	Fri-Sat noon to 10:30 p.m.
Payment:	*Credit cards accepted*
Parking:	*Street parking, can be difficult at night*
Alcohol:	*BYO, no corkage fee*
Atmosphere:	*Casual restaurant*

Don't go to Moti Mahal for its atmosphere (dingy white, with fake roses on the tables and faded posters on the walls). But do go for the food. Moti Mahal's traditional Indian cuisine offers plenty of vegetarian delicacies, such as channa pindi (garbanzo beans) and dum aloo (baby potatoes in a spicy gravy). The lunch buffet, served every day from noon to 3:30 p.m., is a great deal at $6.95. The selection includes aloo samosa (crispy patties stuffed with potatoes), green peas in curry, spinach with cheese, lentils, egg curry, green beans and potatoes, and plenty of basmati rice and yogurt sauce to tone down the spice if necessary. A delicious rice pudding provides a sweet finish. The service, while fairly slow, is adequate. Entrées range from $5.95 to $12.95.

FULL MENU WITH MANY VEGETARIAN OPTIONS

★★ / $$
50. Mysore Woodlands

2548 West Devon Avenue
Chicago, IL 60659
773.338.8160

South Indian

Hours:	Mon-Fri 11:30 a.m. to 9:30 p.m.
	Sat-Sun 11:30 a.m. to 10 p.m.
Payment:	Credit cards accepted
Parking:	Metered street parking, can be challenging on weekends
Alcohol:	BYO, no corkage fee
Atmosphere:	Midscale

Other locations:
See Collar Counties on page 165

If you're used to the usual array of dishes found at most Indian restaurants, you will find some wonderful surprises at Mysore Woodlands, which specializes in the harder-to-find cuisine of southern India. While its all-vegetarian menu contains a few familiar items that you might find anywhere, the better choices (and bigger bargains) are found among the house specialties. Start with one of several varieties of veda (fried lentil doughnuts), alu banda (lentil dumpling with potato and onion), or a bowl of sour and spicy rasam soup ($2.50 to $4.50). For lunch or a simpler dinner, have one of several varieties of uttapam pancakes topped with your choice of onions, chiles, peas, or other vegetables ($6 to $7). Or instead, have a dosai (rice crepe) stuffed with tasty fillings like chutney, potatoes, or lentils ($6 to $12). More ambitious entrées are also available, such as the popular pongal avail featuring mashed rice and lentils in a spicy sauce. If you're very hungry (or in a mood to experiment and share), order a combination thali.

Vegetarian

★★ / $$
51. Orange

3231 North Clark Street
Chicago IL 60657
773.549.4400

MULTIETHNIC

Hours: Daily 8:30 a.m. to 3:00 p.m.
Payment: Credit cards accepted
Parking: Pay lots nearby
Alcohol: BYO, no corkage fee
Atmosphere: Funky breakfast eatery

Other locations:
See Downtown on page 104

Your first clue that this is not your typical breakfast spot probably comes when you pick up the menu, or "menuzine." In addition to three pages of food choices, the menuzine contains articles about things to do in the neighborhood. Orange itself is one of the things to do in this Lakeview neighborhood, or at least one of the places to see and be seen. Crowds wait in line for a table, where they design their own fresh-squeezed juice combos ($3 to $4), with choices including mango, grapefruit, cantaloupe, beet, and, of course, orange. French toast and fruit kabobs ($8.95), Jelly Doughnut Pancakes ($6.95), and grit cakes ($7.95) are the kind of slightly goofy, always tasty fare served up at Orange. The signature dish is Frushi, sushi made with fresh fruit and rice, which is priced daily.

FULL MENU WITH VEGETARIAN AND VEGAN OFFERINGS

★★ / $$
52. Pacific Cafe

1619 North Damen Avenue
Chicago, IL 60647
773.862.1988

PAN-ASIAN

Hours:	Sun-Mon, Wed-Th 11:30 a.m. to 10:00 p.m.
	Fri.-Sat. 11:30 a.m. to 11:00 p.m.
	Closed Tue
Payment:	Credit cards accepted
Parking:	Limited street parking, especially on evenings and weekends
Alcohol:	Beer and wine
Atmosphere:	Midscale

Pacific Cafe, a narrow storefront restaurant in hip Wicker Park, isn't much to look at from the outside. For that matter, with two lines of ordinary square tables and minimally adorned yellow walls, it isn't much to look at from the inside either. But the plain decor belies a giant Pan-Asian menu with plenty of vegetarian items. Appetizers, salads, and entrées are divided into Vietnamese, Thai, and Japanese, and that doesn't even include two pages of maki and sushi. All nonmeat dishes can be made vegan on request; the tempura is egg-less. The light-on-the-rice KaraMaki (make-your-own vegan maki, $4.25) lets you pick up to four ingredients from a list that includes shiitake mushrooms, oshinko mushrooms, cucumber, kampyo, avocado, tempura sweet potato, ohba leaf, tofu, and others, and is not to be missed (although the wasabi is a bit mild). Mix and match with vegan gyoza ($4.95) from Japan, tofu satay ($4.95) from Thailand, and the vegan ginger stir-fry vegetables ($7.75) from Vietnam.

FULL MENU, HEAVY ON SEAFOOD, BUT PLENTY OF VEGETARIAN AND VEGAN ITEMS

★★ / $
53. The Pasta Bowl

>2434 North Clark Street
>Chicago, IL 60614
>773.525.2695
>
>**ITALIAN**
>
>| | |
>|---|---|
>| **Hours:** | Mon-Sat 11:00 a.m. to 11:00 p.m. |
>| | Sun 10:00 a.m. to 10:00 p.m. |
>| **Payment:** | Credit cards accepted |
>| **Parking:** | Street parking can be difficult at night |
>| **Alcohol:** | Full bar |
>| **Atmosphere:** | Casually hip restaurant with counter service |

This laid-back neighborhood restaurant proves two things: decent Italian food need not be expensive, nor must it be bad for you to taste good. Vegetarian offerings include Cappellini Pomodoro ($5.75) and Penne Puttanesca (with marinara, calamata olives, capers, white wine, and oregano, $6.75). And while there are plenty of cream- and cheese-laden dishes, healthier bona vita ("good life") options are available without oil, butter, or cheese. Rounding out the reasonably priced menu are paninis (the "vegetariano" features grilled veggies and a light pesto mayonnaise), salads, and simple appetizers. The staff is friendly and attentive, and entrées can be made without meat upon request. The charmingly decorated narrow room (think bottles of oil on the shelves and low-hanging red lamps) has a long bar where you can watch your food being prepared. Top 40 music plays at conversation-friendly levels.

FULL MENU WITH VEGETARIAN OPTIONS

★★ / $$
54. Pick Me Up Cafe

3408 North Clark Street
Chicago, IL 60657
773.248.6613

AMERICAN

Hours:	Sun-Th 3:00 p.m. to 3:00 a.m. Fri-Sat 24 hours
Payment:	Credit cards accepted
Parking:	Limited street parking, especially during Cubs home games
Alcohol:	No
Atmosphere:	Diner/coffee house

A latticework serving station and tree branches "growing" through the ceiling are meant to give Pick Me Up Café the feel of someone's backyard. Lots of big windows let in enough light to nearly make it feel like you're outside. And despite the fact that it offers fifteen espresso choices ($1.75 to $5), Pick Me Up exudes a decidedly mellow vibe. The restaurant has plenty of vegetarian lunch offerings but does best with its breakfasts and desserts. The Vegan Tofu Scram ($7.25) is a no-nonsense satisfying mix of tomato, onion, mushroom, red and green peppers, potatoes, seared tofu, cilantro, and garlic. The vegan brownie ($2) has the perfect chewy fudge bite (add $1.25 for a la mode with vegan "ice cream"), while the vegan carrot cake ($4) is moist and well frosted. Open till the wee hours, it's the perfect place for a late-night sweet splurge or after-midnight omelet.

FULL MENU WITH MANY VEGETARIAN OFFERINGS

★★★ / $$
55. Ras Dashen

5846 North Broadway
Chicago IL 60660
773.506.9601

ETHIOPIAN

Hours:	Wed-Mon noon to 11:00 p.m. Closed Tue
Payment:	Credit cards accepted
Parking:	Street parking
Alcohol:	Full bar, with several Ethiopian beers
Atmosphere:	Casual, friendly, midscale

Your first decision at Ras Dashen is the choice between traditional seating or more comfy wicker chairs with a short, round wicker table on which your communal meal will arrive. Prepare to dig in with your hands, using the sticky injera bread as your tool (the staff will bring you utensils if you request, but go with tradition). Neophytes should start with the vegetarian combo ($9.95), a selection of five dishes from the vegetarian menu. All of the veg-friendly choices are worth trying, but the miser wat ($8.95), lentils with spicy red pepper sauce, and the shimbera asa wat ($9.95), ground chickpeas made into a dough, are two of the most interesting. All of the restaurant's side dishes, which come with entrées, are vegetarian. The ib (a soft cheese) and the tikil gomen alicha (cabbage, potatoes, and carrots) are nice complements to the vegetarian entrées. The friendly staff is more than willing to make suggestions based on diners' adventure levels and dietary concerns.

FULL MENU WITH MANY VEGETARIAN OFFERINGS

★★ / $$
56. Reza's

5255 North Clark Street
Chicago IL 60640
773.561.1898

MEDITERRANEAN

Hours: Daily 11:00 a.m. to 12:00 p.m.
Payment: Credit cards accepted
Parking: Street parking can be difficult
Alcohol: Full bar
Atmosphere: Midscale, family-friendly

Other locations:
See Downtown on page 108

For vegetarians and carnivores alike, the large menu and large portions at Reza's are legendary. In fact, Reza's is rather legendary as a place that is accessible to Middle Eastern–cuisine neophytes but is authentic enough to attract those who know their hummus from their baba ghanooj. A couple of appetizers are enough for a full meal; an entrée will definitely leave you with leftovers for lunch the next day. Among the items not to miss are the Persian Grilled Potatoes marinated in a house dressing ($3.50), a house specialty cooked just enough to be thoroughly done but not mushy. Also try the Dolmeh Felfel ($3.95), a baked sweet pepper, and the Vegetarian Shami ($3.95), with a pomegranate sauce. The big portions and great big windows looking out on the heart of Andersonville make Reza's a good choice for dining out with a crowd. Food quality doesn't suffer with Reza's excellent delivery service.

FULL MENU WITH MANY VEGETARIAN OFFERINGS

★★★ / $
57. Riques Regional Mexican Food

5004 North Sheridan Road
Chicago, IL 60640
773.728.6200

MEXICAN

Hours:	Daily 11:00 a.m. to 11:00 p.m.
Payment:	Credit cards accepted
Parking:	Street parking can be difficult at night
Alcohol:	BYO, no corkage fee
Atmosphere:	Bright, friendly storefront

The emphasis here is on authentic foods from the many regions of Mexico, meaning you'll find standard tacos and burritos as well as more unusual dishes. In the fall, expect pumpkin-seed sauces and more commonplace tomato, tomatillo, and mole sauces. The cowboy beans have bacon, but the refried beans are vegetarian and are happily not mashed beyond recognition. The chunky guacamole mixes a flavorful salsa-like blend of onions with the avocados. Service is friendly, if not speedy, but the bright yellow decor makes Riques a pleasant place to wait for a cheap meal. Wednesday night specials are all vegetarian: good, but not as packed with flavor as the regular menu. This Uptown/east-of-Andersonville neighborhood is in transition, so dinnertime diners should keep alert when leaving late at night. Entrées range from $4 to $10.

FULL MENU WITH MANY VEGETARIAN OFFERINGS

★★★ / $$
58. Rose Angelis

1314 West Wrightwood Avenue
Chicago, IL 60614
773.296.0081

ITALIAN

Hours:	Tue-Th 5:00 p.m. to 10:00 p.m.
	Fri-Sat 5:00 p.m. to 11:00 p.m.
	Sun 4:30 p.m. to 9:00 p.m.
	Closed Sun
Payment:	Credit cards accepted
Parking:	Street parking can be difficult on weekends
Alcohol:	Full bar
Atmosphere:	Cozy midscale trattoria

A deceptively large restaurant that has long been a Lakeview staple, Rose Angelis has several small- and mid-sized rooms, lending a cozy atmosphere despite the volume of diners. The restaurant isn't the only thing that is large at Rose Angelis; the portion sizes are as well. Special salads ($6.95) come in giant pyramids with layers of seasonal vegetables such as purple potatoes, squash, endive, and peppers. The majority of hearty pasta dishes, including many nightly specials, are veg-friendly. The Mezzalune al Burro ($9.95) is an appealing spinach-stuffed half moon, with pesto that doesn't overwhelm, topped with a sweet brown butter sauce. The attention to detail at Rose Angelis is remarkable. The olive oil on each table is spicy, contributing to an unusual premeal taste. The murals on the wall evoke an authentic, casual Italian cafe. The restaurant even makes its own mozzarella cheese.

**FULL MENU WITH MANY
VEGETARIAN OFFERINGS**

★ / $
59. Royal Thai

2209 West Montrose Avenue
Chicago, IL 60618
773.509.0007

THAI

Hours:	Mon-Tue, Th 11:30 a.m. to 9:30 p.m.
	Fri-Sat 11:30 a.m. to 10:00 p.m.
	Sun noon to 9:00 p.m.
	Closed Wed
Payment:	Credit cards accepted
Parking:	Street parking available
Alcohol:	BYO, no corkage fee
Atmosphere:	Bright, clean, and casual

There is no shortage of Thai restaurants on the North Side, but the eight-table Royal Thai merits vegetarian visits for its extensive offerings. All diners are greeted with two menus: the standard and the vegetarian. The vegetarian menu is not a compromise, boasting more than fifty choices—from traditional options like tom yum soup to a not-to-be-missed wonton and Chinese flowering cabbage soup (both $2.50 or $4.75). Noodle and vegetable dishes are fresh and expertly sauced. The service is as friendly as the "vegetarian welcome" line on the menu suggests. As more upscale restaurants—with typically long waits—open at this intersection of Lincoln, Montrose, and Leavitt, Royal Thai is becoming even more appealing as a simple, neighborhood eatery. Take-out service is available, but not delivery.

VEGETARIAN AND VEGAN OPTIONS

★ / $
60. Sher-a-Punjab Restaurant

2510 West Devon Avenue
Chicago, IL 60659
733.973.4000

INDIAN

Hours:	Daily 11:00 a.m. to 11:00 p.m.
Payment:	Credit cards accepted
Parking:	Metered street parking, can be challenging on weekends
Alcohol:	BYO, no corkage fee
Atmosphere:	Casual family sit-down

Like many Devon Avenue eateries, Sher-a-Punjab isn't much to look at it. Perfectly serviceable, the nondescript pinkish interior sets the stage for a site of good bargains on a street full of bargains. While lunch buffets are the norm at local Indian restaurants, Sher-a-Punjab also has a dinner buffet ($7.95, $6.95 at lunch), so you can get all-you-can-eat any time of day. There's nothing unusual on the buffet menu, but from samosas to the dal, everything is tasty and well-seasoned. Unless you are dining with carnivores, before you head for the buffet line, be sure to tell the waiter that you don't want the platter of tandoori chicken that is typically brought to tables that order the buffet.

**FULL MENU WITH MANY
VEGETARIAN OFFERINGS**

★★ / $
61. Siam Noodle and Rice

4654 North Sheridan Avenue
Chicago, IL 60640
773.769.6694
www.siamnoodleandrice.com

THAI

Hours:	Tue-Th 11:00 a.m. 4:00 p.m., 5:00 p.m. to 9:00 p.m.
	Fri 11:00 a.m. to 4:00 p.m., 5:00 p.m. to 9:30 p.m.
	Sat 11:30 a.m. to 4:00 p.m., 5:00 p.m. to 9:30 p.m.
	Sun 11: 30 a.m. to 4:00 p.m., 5:00 p.m. to 8:00 p.m.
	Closed Mon
Payment:	Credit cards accepted
Parking:	Street parking
Alcohol:	BYO, no corkage fee
Atmosphere:	Family-friendly restaurant/diner

Siam is the definitive hole in the wall, where fifteen simple tables sit under faded Thai tourism posters, and faux-wood wall paneling meets a scuffed linoleum floor, but its legions of fans couldn't care less. They know real-deal homemade food when they taste it. In-the-know Asian families, with grandma there and babies in tow, order ahead and have bountiful feasts served family style. All the usuals (pad thai, tom yum, tom kha kai) are here. Standouts include the pad kee mao (wide noodles and basil) and pad prik mao (string beans, lime leaves, and pepper sauce over rice). The recently added curries are the only dishes that miss the mark. Though many menu items are listed with meat, the waitstaff happily substitutes firm, fresh tofu. Most dishes are around $5, and free Chiclets come with the check.

**FULL MENU WITH MANY
VEGETARIAN OFFERINGS**

★★★ / $
62. Sultan's Market

2057 West North Avenue
Chicago, IL 60647
773.235.3072

MIDDLE EASTERN

Hours:	Mon-Sat 9:00 a.m. to 9:00 p.m.
	Sun 10:00 a.m. to 7:00 p.m.
Payment:	Credit cards accepted
Parking:	Street parking
Alcohol:	No
Atmosphere:	In-store deli/cafe and market

For Middle Eastern food with flare, head to this casual counter-service spot. Booths are roomy and feature the occasional accessory—a stuffed tiger or a hookah. At first you may feel like you're in an Epcot theme restaurant (especially when it's crowded), but rest assured, this is the real deal. A serious salad bar goes beyond typical veggies, including beets, rolled grape leaves, raisins, and more, and fills a large part of the small space. Decked around the bar are Middle Eastern goodies for sale, including fava beans, pine nuts, and authentic candies. Make a meal out of a handful of cheap and entirely vegetarian starters, like Jerusalem salad or baked egg and cheese pie. If you still have room, vegetarian sandwiches (only $3), including classic falafel and zatter fattia (spiced bread with hummus and veggies), are satisfying.

FULL MENU WITH MANY VEGETARIAN AND VEGAN OPTIONS

★★★ / $$
63. Szechuan Garden

> 2901 North Broadway
> Chicago, IL 60657
> 773.525.6677
>
> **CHINESE**
>
> **Hours:** Tue-Sun 12:30 p.m. to 11:00 p.m. Closed Mon
> **Payment:** Credit cards accepted
> **Parking:** Street parking can be a challenge, pay lot across the street
> **Alcohol:** BYO, no corkage fee
> **Atmosphere:** Casual

This serene spot has just seven tables and is a calm oasis in the bustling Lakeview neighborhood. The decor is simple, with soft music and the trickles of a small waterfall drowning out traffic noise. The enormous menu includes at least a hundred vegetarian items, most of them vegan. Some feature soy foods and seitan in otherwise traditional Chinese dishes, like General Tao's soy gluten and kung pao tofu, but standouts are the house specialties, which go well beyond substituting tofu for chicken or beef. More than a dozen vegetarian appetizers include a delicious vegetarian sausage made of yuba (soybean sheets) and walnuts. If you're overwhelmed by the main-dish offerings—all in huge portions— you can't go wrong with Melody on River (soybean crepes filled with taro root and mushroom stuffing, topped with wonderful black bean and garlic chili sauce) or Emerald Bodie Roll (large eggrolls filled with a taro mixture). Chef Ti Fu Wang, who formerly cooked for Buddhist monks in China, is respected for his knowledge of tofu and his perfection with sauces.

FULL MENU SPECIALIZING IN VEGAN DISHES

★★ / $
64. Taste of Lebanon

1509 West Foster Avenue
Chicago, IL 60640
773.334.1600

MIDDLE EASTERN

Hours:	*Mon-Sat 11:00 a.m. to 8:00 p.m.*
Payment:	*Cash only*
Parking:	*Street*
Alcohol:	*BYO, no corkage fee*
Atmosphere:	*Fast food and friendly*

This small, friendly storefront near the heart of Andersonville provides one of the few remaining bargains in an increasingly upscale neighborhood. What Taste of Lebanon lacks in atmosphere, it more than makes up for in flavor and value. Although it doesn't bill itself as a vegetarian restaurant, more than 75 percent of the menu is vegetarian-friendly and mostly vegan. Lebanese standards shine here, including baba ghanooj, hummus, and particularly tasty foul mudamus (fava beans and chickpeas mashed with garlic, parsley, lemon juice, and olive oil). Eschewing the pocket-style sandwich for easy-to-eat wraps, diners will enjoy the slightly spicy falafel sandwich ($2.29). Or try stuffed grape leaves served in a sandwich with or without hummus. Lentil soup, several salads, and homemade Lebanese-style yogurt are also available. If you're ravenous, two generously proportioned vegetarian combinations are available, which, at just $4.99, will fill you up without emptying your wallet.

MOSTLY VEGETARIAN, SOME VEGAN

★★ / $
65. Tel Aviv Kosher Pizza

6349 North California Avenue
Chicago, IL 60659
773.764.3776

MULTIETHNIC

Hours:	Mon-Th 11:00 a.m. to 11:00 p.m.
	Fri 11:00 a.m. to 2:00 p.m. (winter),
	11:00 a.m. to 3:00 p.m. (summer)
	Sat 2 hours after sundown to 1:00 a.m.
Payment:	Cash only (ATM down the street)
Parking:	Street parking possible
Alcohol:	No
Atmosphere:	Counter service and take-out joint

From the banter across the counter as you place your order, to the lively discussions you'll overhear at the tables (e.g., the state of the Israeli stock market, gay marriage, and the logistics of throwing it all in and moving to Las Vegas), Tel Aviv Kosher Pizza is one of those instantly comfortable neighborhood hangouts. With far more than pizza (thick and thin crust) on its kosher (including dairy and fish, but no meat) menu, vegetarians can choose from egg salad sandwiches, Mexican entrées, chili, salads, Chinese food, Middle Eastern treats, and, of course, Italian dishes and pizza. Even the chocolate brownies are good, if dense. The menu includes an ample selection of dishes under $3, with the top end near $7. Tel Aviv is strictly fast food with no frills, but it is clean, friendly, flavorful, and the slices of pizza hold their own in a city that loves its pizza. Smoking is not permitted. Delivery service is available.

VEGETARIAN; FISH ALSO SERVED

★★ / $$
66. Tiffin, the Indian Kitchen

2536 West Devon Avenue
Chicago, IL 60659
773.338.2143

INDIAN/PAKISTANI

Hours:	Mon-Fri 11:30 a.m. to 3:00 p.m., Mon-Fri 5:00 p.m. to 10:00 p.m. Sat-Sun 11:30 a.m. to 10:00 p.m.
Payment:	Credit cards accepted
Parking:	Street parking, can be challenging on weekend nights; valet available Friday to Sunday
Alcohol:	Full bar
Atmosphere:	Upscale, sophisticated full-service restaurant

Even locals who rarely make it to Devon Avenue for authentic Indian food know Tiffin. Perhaps the strip's best-known restaurant, Tiffin may also be its most upscale and expensive. From the dim lighting to the suited servers to the artful recessed ceiling painted with blue skies and clouds, Tiffin elevates the typical casual Indian restaurant experience. Traditional Indian dishes from both northern and southern India are consistently good and worth the higher prices. For a change of pace from traditional naan, Tiffin offers ten different Indian breads. The weekday lunch buffet ($8) is a less expensive way to sample Tiffin's cuisine. On weekends, Tiffin is always crowded, and reservations are recommended. Service is professional but can be slow at times, so expect a leisurely meal.

FULL MENU WITH MANY VEGETARIAN OFFERINGS

★★ / $
67. Udupi Palace

2543 West Devon Avenue
Chicago, IL 60618
773.338.2152
www.udupipalace.com

South Indian

Hours:	Mon-Th 11:30 a.m. to 9:30 p.m.
	Fri-Sat 11:30 a.m. to 10:00 p.m.
	Sun 11:30 a.m. to 9:30 p.m.
Payment:	Credit cards accepted
Parking:	Metered street parking, can be challenging on weekends
Alcohol:	BYO, no corkage fee
Atmosphere:	Casual, long-standing favorite

Other locations:
See Suburban Cook County on page 157

Udupi Palace is consistently named as a favorite among the many vegetarian restaurants that dot Devon Avenue. A recent remodel has made the South Indian eatery more inviting, with dark wood tables and light wood floors, while the menu has remained above average. Instead of the typical all-you-can-eat Indian buffets, Udupi offers reasonably priced lunch specials ($5.95 to $7.95), as well as dishes from its ample and moderately priced menu. Save the pappadam ($1.50) for another restaurant. It is bland and uninteresting. Instead, try the mulligatawny soup with lentils or one of the several special thalis. The pullav rice dishes are a tasty alternative to lentils and dosai, although the dosai is a solid performer here, too.

VEGETARIAN AND SOME VEGAN OPTIONS

★★★ / $$

68. Uncommon Ground Coffeehouse and Cafe

1214 West Grace Street
Chicago, IL 60613
773.929.3680
www.uncommonground.com

MULTIETHNIC

Hours:	Sun-Th 9:00 a.m. to 11:00 p.m.
	Fri-Sat 9:00 a.m. to midnight
Payment:	Credit cards accepted
Parking:	Street parking possible except during Cubs games
Alcohol:	Full bar
Atmosphere:	Coffee klatch

With its exposed brick walls, fireplace, and comfy window seats, Uncommon Ground is an inviting coffeehouse. It is the kind of place where nationally known live musicians raise money for breast cancer research, and locals sit at outdoor tables with their dogs on late summer evenings. The menu is more extensive than the more common coffee shop. Sure, there are the basics like pita and hummus, but the menu is also filled with culinary-school-quality dishes. Vegetarian chili, a Thai vegetable salad, pizzas, and a sun-dried tomato pesto risotto are among the best bets for vegetarians. The pumpkin ravioli is so good that people crave it year-round, not just in the traditional pumpkin season of fall. Even the veggie burger here is more flavorful than most. At least two-thirds of the menu is veg-friendly, so there are few dishes that are off limits. Uncommon Ground was one of the city's first smoke-free coffeehouses. Entrées range from $7 to $16.

VEGETARIAN; MEAT AND FISH ALSO SERVED

★★★ / $$
69. Unique So Chique

4600 North Magnolia Avenue
(entrance on Wilson, next to Starbucks)
Chicago, IL 60640
773.561.0324
www.uniquesochique.com

MULTIETHNIC

Hours:	Tue-Fri 11:30 a.m. to 8:00 p.m.
	Sat 10:00 a.m. to 8:00 p.m.
	Sun 10:00 a.m. to 5:00 p.m.
	Closed Mon
Payment:	Credit cards accepted
Parking:	Street parking can be difficult weekends
Alcohol:	No
Atmosphere:	Retail store tea shop

You'll likely walk right by Unique So Chique for two reasons. First, despite its Magnolia Avenue address, the entrance is on Wilson Avenue. Second, this tiny tearoom and chocolate parlor is hidden in the back of a retail shop, making it nearly invisible to the naked eye. But this charming Uptown nook is worth the search. The lunch menu contains an interesting selection of vegetarian options, including sandwiches made of cucumber and roma tomato ($7.95), avocado and sprouts ($7.95), and brie and cumin ($8.95), plus pizzas such as a rosemary and wild mushroom ($14.95). The weekend brunch offers a tempting selection of omelettes with scalloped potatoes and fresh-baked bread. Being a chocolate room as well as a tearoom, you are almost obliged to save room for fudge or freshly baked desserts with a cup of tea.

FULL MENU WITH MANY VEGETARIAN OPTIONS

★★★ / $$
70. Victory's Banner

2100 West Roscoe Street
Chicago, IL 60618
773.665.0227

MULTIETHNIC

Hours:	*Wed-Sun 8:00 a.m. to 3:00 p.m.*
	Closed Tue
Payment:	*Credit cards accepted*
Parking:	*Street parking possible*
Alcohol:	*No*
Atmosphere:	*Spiritually themed, casual sit-down*

From the demeanor of the waitstaff, to the New Age music, to the soothing paint colors, there's something inherently calming about Victory's Banner. By the time you've enjoyed fresh-squeezed orange juice, French toast with peach butter, or a Veggie Delight omelette with soy sausage, it is like you've gone on a mini relaxation retreat. Even as crowds snake out the door on weekend mornings (and they always do), the staff, inspired by Indian Spiritual Master Sri Chinmoy, keeps things orderly. Even those who are strictly secular rave about the food, which includes free-range eggs (and vegan Eggless Wonders), three kinds of veggie burgers, pizzas, salads, Neatloaf (a meat-free meatloaf), and other dishes, all with creative combinations of ingredients and spices. Prices range from $4.75 to $7.95. The restaurant is nonsmoking and offers take-out service, but the ambiance is (almost) as good as that peach butter, so it is worth the wait to eat in.

VEGETARIAN WITH MANY VEGAN OFFERINGS

★ / $
71. Yes Thai

> 5211 North Damen Avenue
> Chicago, IL 60625
> 773.878.3487
> *www.yesthaicuisine.com*
>
> **THAI**
>
> | | |
> |---|---|
> | **Hours:** | Mon-Th 11:30 a.m. to 9:30 p.m. |
> | | Fri-Sat 11:30 a.m. to 10:30 p.m. |
> | | Sun 3:00 to 9:00 p.m. |
> | **Payment:** | Credit cards accepted |
> | **Parking:** | Street parking |
> | **Alcohol:** | BYO, no corkage fee |
> | **Atmosphere:** | Casual, bright restaurant |

This bright, sunny spot is a welcome addition to an otherwise boring strip of Damen Avenue. Fresh, tasty food and speedy service—almost always with a smile—have made it a fast favorite with many in the neighborhood. Standouts from typical Thai fare include the crispy tofu appetizer ($3) garnished with crushed peanuts and accompanied by a sweet-and-sour sauce, and the rama special ($6), crunchy steamed broccoli and fresh ginger served with a yummy house-made peanut sauce over rice. The pad thai and pad see eiw (each $6), often served with a yawn at other Thai restaurants, are bright in flavor and presentation. Curries are on the soupy side, but tasty nonetheless. All entrées can be prepared with tofu or extra vegetables, and weekday dine-in lunch specials include an appetizer and entrée for just $5.75—one of the best deals in town. An added bonus: there's free wireless Internet access Mon-Sat until 5:30 p.m. An outdoor patio is open in warm weather and home delivery service tends to be quick.

FULL MENU WITH MANY VEGETARIAN OFFERINGS

Downtown

★★ / $$
1. Artopolis Bakery, Cafe, and Agora

306 South Halsted Street
Chicago, IL 60661
312.559.9000

GREEK

Hours:	Sun-Th 9:00 a.m. to 11:00 p.m.
	Fri-Sat 9:00 a.m. to midnight
Payment:	Credit cards accepted
Parking:	Street parking possible
Alcohol:	Full bar
Atmosphere:	Casual

Taking its name from the Greek words *artos* (bread) and *polis* (town), Artopolis offers an appealing alternative to the more traditional restaurants dotting the streets of Greektown. With an on-site bakery, it would be easy to never move beyond the delicious bread and impressive array of desserts (fruit tarts, baklava, lokouamades, and Greek cookies, just to name a few). But those seeking something more substantial won't be disappointed. Favorite starters include melinzana crostini (essentially an eggplant bruschetta), and an interesting spinach salad with sesame goat cheese ($5.75 to 8.25). The sandwich menu highlights the bread offerings nicely, with such choices as the Capricciozo (tomato, Kasseri cheese, basil, and garlic olive tapenade on cheese focaccia) and the Portobello Chevre (portobello mushrooms, peppers, marinated onions, and goat cheese on sun-dried tomato boule). As a sandwich alternative, Artopolis also offers "Artopitas," their own brand of Greek-style filled pies. Finally, a surprising find on the menu is a huge selection of Mediterranean pizzas with a variety of cheeses and roasted vegetables. In addition to the full bar, juices, sodas, tea, and traditional Greek coffees are also offered.

FULL MENU WITH MANY VEGETARIAN OPTIONS

★ / $
2. Bialy Cafe

1421 West Chicago Avenue
Chicago, IL 60622
312.733.7165

MEXICAN/AMERICAN

Hours:	Mon-Fri 7:00 a.m. to 8:00 p.m.
	Sat 7:00 a.m. to 6:00 p.m.
	Sun 7:00 a.m. to 5:00 p.m.
Payment:	Credit cards accepted
Parking:	Metered street parking
Alcohol:	No
Atmosphere:	Coffee shop

An unassuming diner on a strip of Chicago Avenue that is increasingly becoming a destination for above-average eating, Bialy Cafe is reminiscent of the East Village's past. Looking like hundreds, if not thousands, of average luncheonettes in Chicago, Bialy Cafe's Mexican-inspired menu is a pleasant surprise to vegetarians. The Chilaquese ($4.95), Mexican omelette ($4.55), portobello burrito ($5.95), and avocado club ($5.95) are all flavorful, large-portion options for the price of most fast food. Some of the Mexican dishes tend to be spicy—a welcome addition for some but cause for warning for others. Look for some unexpected additions to otherwise traditional recipes, such as broccoli in the nachos. Because of the heavy Mexican influence at Bialy Cafe, most dishes have cheese and would not be suitable for vegan diners.

FULL MENU WITH MANY VEGETARIAN OFFERINGS

★★★★ / $$$
3. Crofton on Wells

535 North Wells Street
Chicago, IL 60610
312.755.1790
www.croftononwells.com

AMERICAN REGIONAL

Hours:	Mon-Th 5:00 p.m. to 10:00 p.m.
	Fri-Sat 5:00 p.m. to 11:00 p.m.
	Closed Sun
Payment:	Credit cards accepted
Parking:	Valet, metered street parking can be difficult
Alcohol:	Full bar with more than 150 wines
Atmosphere:	Upscale, elegant but minimalist

Chef Suzy Crofton has cooked at Le Francais in Wheeling and Montparnasse in Naperville, but at her namesake restaurant she's earned the allegiance of local vegetarians. The understated decor makes Crofton on Wells good for anything from a first date to a client dinner. In addition to her regular menu, a seasonal menu accommodates both vegans and vegetarians; Crofton has a separate smaller menu of vegetarian items available by request. Thick organic Japanese miso broth is more a meal than a mere soup, with its ginger, buckwheat soba noodles, and roasted seasonal vegetables ($17). The risotto appetizer, with chanterelles, buttercup squash, sage pesto, and Chaubier cheese ($10.25) topped with toasted pumpkin seeds, is also a winner. The menu changes seasonally, so expect to be pleasantly surprised each time you go. The staff is professional and accommodating for special requests.

FULL MENU WITH MANY VEGETARIAN AND VEGAN OFFERINGS

★★ / $$
4. Flat Top Grill

1000 West Washington Boulevard
Chicago, IL 60607
312.829.4800

PAN-ASIAN

Hours:	Mon-Th 11:00 a.m. to 9:30 p.m.
	Fri-Sat 11:00 a.m. to 10:30 p.m.
	Sun noon to 9:00 p.m.
Payment:	Credit cards accepted
Parking:	Valet, nearby pay lot, street parking challenging on weekdays
Alcohol:	Full bar
Atmosphere:	Midscale, DIY chain

Other locations:
See North Side on page 40; Suburban Cook County on page 143

This make-your-own stir-fry chain is a great place to take the whole brood. Grab a bowl from the stir-fry bar and fill it with your choice of rice, noodles, and fresh vegetables, then top it off with a few ladles from the selection of sauces (meat and fish eaters can also fill a side dish with beef, chicken, or seafood). Add a color-coded stick to turn your stir-fry into a wrap or soup, have it piled atop a bed of greens, or request it be cooked in a separate wok to avoid cross-contamination. The selection of ingredients changes quarterly to reflect local growing seasons. There's also a small menu of Asian-inspired appetizers, plus martinis and fruity tropical drinks. Unlimited trips to the stir-fry bar cost $7.99 at lunch and $12.99 at dinner for adults; meals for children ten and under are $4.99.

VEGETARIAN AND VEGAN OFFERINGS; MEAT, FISH, POULTRY, AND SEAFOOD ALSO SERVED

★★ / $$
5. Flo

1434 West Chicago Avenue
Chicago, IL 60622
312.243.0477

NEW MEXICAN

Hours:	Tue-Th 8:30 a.m. to 2:30 p.m., 5:30 p.m. to 10:00 p.m.
	Fri 8:30 a.m. to 2:30 p.m., 5:30 p.m. to 11:00 p.m.
	Sat 9:00 a.m. to 2:30 p.m., 5:30 p.m. to 11:00 p.m.
	Sun 9:00 a.m. to 2:30 p.m.
	Closed Mon
Payment:	Credit cards accepted
Parking:	Metered street parking
Alcohol:	Full bar
Atmosphere:	Bright, arty cafe with a twist

Once a little-known brunch-only spot in an oft-overlooked neighborhood, Flo is now a hipster hangout. The New Mexican cuisine relies heavily on eggs and cheeses, so there's virtually nothing on the menu to please vegans. But the variety of egg dishes—many named after Flo—are sure to satisfy vegetarians at breakfast. Favorites include Flo-style eggs ($5.95), served with roasted poblano sauce and black beans, and the chilaquiles ($6.95), scrambled eggs with cheddar cheese and pico de gallo. Polenta hash ($7.95) mixes roasted garlic, sautéed mushrooms, squash, and red peppers in a poblano sauce. Flo is now open for lunch and dinner, but breakfast and brunch remain the popular mainstay. Expect a wait.

FULL MENU WITH MANY VEGETARIAN OFFERINGS

★★ / $
6. Foodlife

Water Tower Place, Mezzanine
835 North Michigan Avenue
Chicago, IL 60611
312.335.3663
www.leye.com

MULTIETHNIC

Hours:	*Sun-Th 11:00 a.m. to 8:00 p.m.*
	Fri-Sat 11:00 a.m. to 9:00 p.m.
Market:	*Mon-Sat 10:00 a.m. to 8:00 p.m.*
	Sun 11:00 a.m. to 7:00 p.m.
Payment:	*Credit cards accepted*
Parking:	*Expensive pay lot*
Alcohol:	*No*
Atmosphere:	*Healthy, tourist-friendly food court*

Water Tower Place is most famous for its seven floors of shopping, but at the base of it all is this ethnically oriented, health-conscious food court owned by corporate restaurant powerhouse Lettuce Entertain You. Unlike free-for-all food courts, here a hostess seats you and marks your table reserved, allowing you to leisurely choose among the thirteen stations. Summertime tourism means long lines, but the 600-seat space ensures a short wait, and despite the size and controlled chaos, the garden-like setting is cute and cozy. Vegetarians get great options from Vida Mexicana, serving veggie and bean burritos; Stir Fry Heaven, with vegetable pot stickers, tofu pad Thai, and a vegan mushroom broth for stir-frying broccoli, bok choy, pea pods, bean sprouts, and more. The Souplife kiosk offers eight flavors, including a vegetarian chili, and a smoothie station mixes fruit drinks as well as organic carrot juice. Finish with a dessert crepe, gelato, or brownie from Sweet Life. Meals $6 to $12.

FULL MENU WITH MANY VEGETARIAN OPTIONS AND SOME VEGAN OPTIONS

★★ / $
7. Fresh Choice

1534 North Wells Street
Chicago, IL 60610
312.664.7065

MULTIETHNIC

Hours:	Daily 8:00 a.m. to 10:00 p.m.
	Daily 8:00 a.m. to midnight (summer hours)
Payment:	Cash only
Parking:	Street parking and pay lot
Alcohol:	No
Atmosphere:	Take-out spot with juice bar

Other locations:
233 North Michigan Avenue, Chicago, IL 60601
　312.856.1454
See North Side on page 42

Who knew comfort food could be so good for you? With a menu including beverages that allow you to add nutritious "hits"—from brewer's yeast to bee pollen—this Old Town storefront shop accomplishes it. The menu boasts healthy options such as soups, subs, salads, and baked potatoes with a variety of toppings, all in the $2.50 to $6.75 range. The veggie sub ($5.45), with vegetables and three cheeses on warm crusty bread, is as filling as its meaty counterparts. Fresh Choice's true claims to fame are its smoothies, which are made with either skim milk or fresh fruit juice; they are tasty albeit pricey ($3.42). The cozy decor is that of a local hangout, with counter service and white boards serving as menus. Bright yellow walls contrasting with the whir of a blender complete the picture.

FULL MENU WITH MANY VEGETARIAN OPTIONS

★ / $$
8. Gaylord India

678 North Clark Street
Chicago, IL 60610
312.664.1700

INDIAN

Hours:	Mon-Sun 11:30 a.m. to 2:30 p.m. 5:30 p.m. to 9:30 p.m.
Payment:	Credit cards accepted
Parking:	Valet ($9)
Alcohol:	Yes
Atmosphere:	More upscale than most Indian buffets

There are too many affordable, edible, vegetarian-friendly Indian buffets to count along Devon Avenue (see North Side). But in this area of downtown, just west of the Magnificent Mile, an affordable meal of any sort is worth a note. Gaylord India, which has been a mainstay of the area for nearly thirty years, serves an extensive, above-average lunch buffet with an array of dishes, including vegetarian options like sag paneer (spinach with cheese), bhindi (deep-fried okra), and vegetable curry. The regular menu features more meat dishes than many Indian restaurants, but the vegetarian-friendly items are ample and flavorful. The sit-down service can be spotty, so don't head to Gaylord when you're in a hurry. Plus, with buffet, you'll want time to be able to go back for seconds. Most vegetarian entrées are $7.95.

VEGETARIAN AND VEGAN OFFERINGS; MEAT, FISH, POULTRY, AND SEAFOOD ALSO SERVED

★★★ / $$$
9. Gioco

1312 South Wabash Avenue
Chicago, IL 60605
312.939.3870
www.gioco-chicago.com

CONTEMPORARY ITALIAN

Hours:	Mon-Fri 11:00 a.m. to 2:00 p.m.
	Mon-Wed 5:00 p.m. to 10:00 p.m.
	Th 5:00 p.m. to 11:00 p.m.
	Fri-Sat 5:00 p.m. to midnight
	Sun 5:00 p.m. to 10:00 p.m.
Payment:	Credit cards accepted
Parking:	Street parking, valet
Alcohol:	Full bar
Atmosphere:	Trendy and upscale

At first glance this hip restaurant in the rapidly gentrifying South Loop might not seem like a good spot for vegetarians. In fact, main-course vegetarian options are exclusively on the primi section of the menu, as all second-course items are meat-based. But this shouldn't be seen as a compromise. The ricotta and spinach tortellini in a butter, sage, and pecorino sauce ($15) is deliciously rich. The tagliatelle ai funghi porcini features wide ribbon noodles in a creamy sauce with bits of porcini mushrooms. There's also a selection of vegetarian-friendly pizzas. The five contorni (vegetable side dishes) include roasted brussels sprouts ($6) prepared with olive oil, butter, and salt, that are tender and delicious enough to win over even the most ardent opponent to this sometimes bitter vegetable. Often prepared with both olive oil and butter, Gioco's dishes tend to be rich and filling (and not suitable for vegans), but the ingredients are fresh and the preparations superb.

**FULL MENU WITH MANY
VEGETARIAN OFFERINGS**

★★★★ / $$$
10. Green Zebra

1460 West Chicago Avenue
Chicago, IL 60622
312.243.7100

CONTEMPORARY AMERICAN

Hours:	Tue-Th 5:30 p.m. to 10:00 p.m.
	Fri-Sat 5:30 p.m. to 11:00 p.m.
	Sun 5:30 p.m. to 9:00 p.m.
	Closed Mon
Payment:	Credit cards accepted
Parking:	Metered street parking possible, valet
Alcohol:	Full bar
Atmosphere:	Minimalist, yet swanky and eco-friendly

To say that Chicago vegetarians have been waiting for Green Zebra with bated breath is not an exaggeration. For much of 2003 and 2004 the question on everyone's lips was, "When's Shawn's place going to open?" Shawn being Shawn McClain, owner and chef of the popular (but not vegetarian-friendly) Spring. Green Zebra, named after the heirloom tomato, is one of those rare restaurants that deserves the hype. An almost entirely vegetarian menu plays off the tapas/small plates concepts, so diners can easily sample the frequently changing seasonal creations. The Oregon Morel Mushroom and Spring Onion Galette ($11) and Spicy Scallion Pancakes in a stack with kimchee ($7) are favorites. Several other dishes, such as Nonna Zanella's Potato Gnocchi ($10), are inspired by other local chefs. While pricier enough to constitute a night on the town, the way the menu is structured makes it accessible to those on a budget. Plan an evening to relax and enjoy. And save room for dessert.

VEGETARIAN AND VEGAN MENU; LIMITED MEAT, FISH, POULTRY, AND SEAFOOD ALSO SERVED

★★ / $$
11. India House

59 West Grand Avenue
Chicago IL 60610
312.645.9500

INDIAN

Hours:	Mon-Th 11:00 a.m. to 2:30 p.m., 5:00 p.m. to 10:00 p.m.
	Fri 11:00 a.m. to 2:30 p.m., 5:00 p.m. to 11:00 p.m.
	Sat 11:00 a.m. to 3:00 p.m. 5:00 p.m. to 11:00 p.m.
	Sun 11:00 a.m. to 3:00 p.m. 5:00 p.m. to 10:00 p.m.
Payment:	Credit cards accepted
Parking:	Valet, pay lot
Alcohol:	Full bar
Atmosphere:	Family-friendly sit-down

Other locations:
See Suburban Cook County on page 145

While not lavish, this restaurant is a step up from many Devon Avenue eateries, with its linen napkins and tablecloths as well as a staff more attentive than most. The large menu contains pages of both meat and vegetarian fare, with vegetable specialties clearly marked. The aloo paratha ($4) disappoints traditionalists, as the potato is "baked in with the spices" instead of the more standard stuffed bread. Otherwise, most dishes, including tandoori vegetables ($10.95), chili pakora ($4), and dal makhani ($11.95), meet expectations and are served to requested spice level. Try something off of the "Chaupati Corner" menu, which features "Bombay Street Fare." A children's menu has small portions of the milder Indian foods as well as American foods for those whose young ones aren't as adventuresome.

FULL MENU WITH MANY VEGETARIAN AND VEGAN OFFERINGS

★ / $
12. Jubilee Juice

> 140 North Halsted Street
> Chicago, IL 60661
> 312.491.8500
> www.jubileejuice.com
>
> **MULTIETHNIC**
>
> | | |
> |---|---|
> | Hours: | Mon-Fri 9:00 a.m. to 10 p.m. |
> | | Fri-Sat 10:00 a.m. to 10:00 p.m. |
> | | Closed Sun |
> | Payment: | Credit cards accepted |
> | Parking: | Street possible |
> | Alcohol: | No |
> | Atmosphere: | No-frills takeout |

Besides more than twenty smoothie and fresh-squeezed juice options, there's a good selection of soups, salads, baked potatoes, and vegetarian sandwiches at this West Loop spot. Standouts include the Greek Salad Sandwich as well as the BBQ Baja Salad, which has avocado, corn, black beans, and tomatoes topped with a creamy barbeque dressing. Meat eaters will find plenty to choose from, too, including burgers, chicken, and fish sandwiches. Waffle fries please pretty much everyone. There are some tables in the small dining space, but the bulk of the business here is takeout.

FULL MENU WITH VEGETARIAN OFFERINGS

★★ / $$
13. Klay Oven

414 North Orleans Street
Chicago, IL 60610
312.527.3999

INDIAN

Hours:	Mon-Fri 11:30 a.m. to 2:30 p.m., 5:30 p.m. to 10:00 p.m. Sat-Sun noon to 3:00 p.m., 5:30 p.m. to 10:00 p.m.
Payment:	Credit cards accepted
Parking:	Street
Alcohol:	Full bar
Atmosphere:	Upscale

Elegant wall hangings, subdued lighting, and draped windows create a pretty setting for upscale Indian in River North. Weekday lunches attract a chattering crowd of coworkers for the inexpensive Indian buffet, offering a high-quality selection of vegetable and meat dishes as well as steaming rice and hot quarters of lightly buttered naan bread. At dinner, the mood mellows with a romantic candlelit atmosphere. Start with beautifully formed, puffed vegetable samosas, deep fried and kicky. An entire entrée category is devoted to vegetarian options such as Palak Paneer, homemade cheese balls with braised spinach and delicate spices. Paneer Rasmissa mixes mild cheese with rich tomato-based sauce. An order of basmati rice is enough for two or three to share and provides a perfect balance. Friendly English-speaking servers can help with menu decisions and appropriate chutneys. Try an Indian beer like Taj Mahal or King Fisher to accompany your meal. Entrées $7 to $12.

FULL MENU WITH MANY VEGETARIAN AND VEGAN DISHES

★★ / $$
14. Leona's

646 North Franklin Street
Chicago, IL 60610
312.867.0101
www.leonas.com

ITALIAN, AMERICAN

Hours: Mon-Th 11:00 a.m. to 10:30 p.m.
Fri-Sat 11:00 a.m. to 11:30 p.m.
Sun noon to 10:00 p.m.
Payment: Credit cards accepted
Parking: Street parking difficult, nearby lot after 5:00 p.m.
Alcohol: Full bar, including organic beer and wine
Atmosphere: Family-friendly midscale

Other locations:
1419 West Taylor Street, Chicago, IL 60607, 312.850.2222
See also North Side on page 56; South Side on page 125; Suburban Cook County on page 149

Leona's bills itself as a "closet vegetarian" joint with an emphasis on fresh, wholesome ingredients. In other words, no "frankenfoods." So dig in reassuringly to the portobello and white mushrooms in whole wheat ravioli; vegan burger made of tofu, sliced mushrooms, sunflower seeds, and rolled oats; and grilled flatbread wraps stuffed with tofu, roasted veggies, or hummus. The deep-dish pizza ($21.50 for a large) reigns supreme, made with a touch of cornmeal in the crust. Imaginative toppings include pesto or hummus instead of typical tomato sauce. Soy cheese can be substituted for any other cheese. Entrées range from $11 to $25 and pasta/sandwiches/burgers from $8.50 to $13.

FULL MENU WITH MANY VEGETARIAN AND VEGAN OFFERINGS

★ / $
15. Lo Cal Zone

912 North Rush Street
Chicago, IL 60611
312.943.9060

MULTIETHNIC

Hours:	Mon-Th 11:00 a.m. to 10:00 p.m.
	Fri-Sat 11:00 a.m. to 11:00 p.m.
	Sun noon to 10:00 p.m.
Payment:	Cash only
Parking:	Pay lots nearby
Alcohol:	No
Atmosphere:	Take-out lunch spot

This shack in the middle of a parking lot just west of Magnificent Mile is easy to miss, and, frankly, looks like something you might want to just pass on by. But if you work in the Streeterville area or just don't want to spend the king's ransom most area eateries charge for a quick bite, stop in. There are a few stools at tall tables for eat-in dining, but the bulk of business is takeout. A wrap sandwich ($5.50), veggie burger ($4.95), and veggie chili ($2.55 or $3.55) are among the most solidly flavorful and veg-friendly options on the menu board. The service is fast and friendly; the line moves quickly.

**FULL MENU WITH MANY
VEGETARIAN OFFERINGS**

★★ / $
16. Mac Kelly's Greens and Things

177 North Wells Street
Chicago, IL 60606
312.899.9022

AMERICAN SALAD BAR

Hours: Mon-Fri 6:30 a.m. to 3:00 p.m.
Payment: Cash and checks accepted
Parking: Pay lots nearby
Alcohol: No
Atmosphere: Take-out lunch spot

Other locations:
225 North Michigan Avenue, Chicago, IL 60601
   312.540.0071
123 West Madison Avenue, Chicago, IL 60602
   312.214.6401
77 East Madison Avenue, Chicago, IL 60602
   312.346.8072
21 East Adams Street, Chicago, IL 60603
   312.431.1373

Downtown workers who dine at their desks love this totally take-out spot. A cold sandwich bar includes pasta, tuna, and faux crab salads. The refrigerated section offers yogurts, fresh fruit, juices, and soda. But the main draw is the mammoth, U-shaped salad bar, kept surprisingly clean and refreshed throughout the day. Suitable for both vegetarians and carnivorous friends, it boasts nearly eighty items, starting with four types of greens and ending with twelve different dressings. A hot bar (typically closed by 2:00 p.m.) offers a few options for vegetarians, such as baked potatoes, soups, macaroni and cheese, and steamed veggies, but vegans should approach with caution, as most are doused in butter. Salad/sandwich bar $4.99/pound; hot items $2.75 to $6.99.

FULL MENU WITH MANY VEGETARIAN AND VEGAN OFFERINGS

★ / $
17. Oasis Cafe

21 North Wabash Street
  (located in back of Jeweler's Mall)
Chicago, IL 60602
312.558.1098

MIDDLE EASTERN

Hours:	Mon-Sat 10:00 a.m. to 5:00 p.m.
Payment:	Credit cards accepted
Parking:	Street parking difficult, many nearby pay lots
Alcohol:	No
Atmosphere:	Fast food

Tucked away in an unlikely spot at the back of the Wabash Jeweler's Mall, Oasis Cafe serves a small but diverse menu of Middle Eastern favorites. Most of the standards are here, including falafel (sandwiches or straight up), baba ghanooj, tabbouleh, and hummus. But you'll also find slightly less common offerings, like a delicately flavored, stew-like foul (fava beans), the Egyptian Salad with chickpeas ($5.39), or the grilled eggplant sandwich ($3.49). Although the specials often skew towards the meat side of the menu, some of the tastier vegetarian options also put in an appearance as semi-regulars, like stuffed grape leaves, a portobello mushroom sandwich, and vegetarian Moroccan couscous ($4.39 to $6.39). Relatively inexpensive, especially by downtown standards, there's nothing on this menu that you'll feel you can't afford, even if you've just dropped two months' salary on an engagement ring.

FULL MENU WITH MANY VEGETARIAN OPTIONS

★ / $
18. Old Jerusalem

>1411 North Wells Street
>Chicago, IL 60610
>312.944.0459

>**MIDDLE EASTERN**

>Hours: *Daily 11:00 a.m. to 11:00 p.m.*
>Payment: *Credit cards accepted*
>Parking: *Street parking difficult or pay lot*
>Alcohol: *BYO, corkage fee $1 per person*
>Atmosphere: *Casual hole-in-the-wall*

This nondescript Old Town spot doesn't stand out among its more upscale, trendy Wells Street neighbors, but since 1976 it has scored points for reliably good Middle Eastern food—no fusion, no fuss. The decor (exposed brick walls, ceiling fans, dim lighting) is simple, and the service is somewhat slight. The food is standard fare from hummus to baklava, fresh and tasty. Appetizers ($2.95 to $4.25) include tabbouleh, Jerusalem salad, and stuffed grape leaves. Follow your starter with one of nine vegetarian entrées, from a typical Greek salad ($5.95) to foul (fava beans with garlic and lemon, $6.95). The falafel is perfectly crispy, not too greasy, and comes with a generous serving of tahini. When warmer temperatures hit, head to the street-front patio, a bottle of wine in tow.

FULL MENU WITH MANY VEGETARIAN OPTIONS

★★ / $$
19. Orange

75 West Harrison Street
Chicago, IL 60605
312.447.1000

MULTIETHNIC

Hours:	Daily 8:30 a.m. to 3:00 p.m.
Payment:	Credit cards accepted
Parking:	Pay lots nearby
Alcohol:	BYO, no corkage fee
Atmosphere:	Funky breakfast eatery

Other locations:
See North Side on page 64

Your first clue that this is not your typical breakfast spot probably comes when you pick up the menu, or "menuzine." In addition to three pages of food choices, it contains articles about things to do in the neighborhood. Orange itself is one of the things to do in this South Loop neighborhood, or at least one of the places to see and be seen. Diners design their own fresh-squeezed juice combos ($3 to $4), with choices including mango, grapefruit, cantaloupe, beet, and, of course, orange. French toast and fruit kabobs ($8.95), Jelly Doughnut Pancakes ($6.95), and grit cakes ($7.95) are the kind of slightly goofy, always tasty fare served up at Orange. The signature dish is Frushi, sushi made with fresh fruit and rice, which is priced daily.

**FULL MENU WITH VEGETARIAN
AND VEGAN OFFERINGS**

★ / $$
20. Pegasus

130 South Halsted Street
Chicago, IL 60606
312.226.3377

GREEK

Hours:	Mon-Th 11:00 a.m. to midnight
	Fri 11:00 a.m. to 1:00 a.m.
	Sat noon to 1:00 a.m.
	Sun noon to midnight
Payment:	Credit cards accepted
Parking:	Street parking possible, pay lot nearby
Alcohol:	Full bar
Atmosphere:	Family-friendly sit-down

This large, loud restaurant has an extensive menu featuring hot appetizers such as saganaki ($4.50), the famous flaming cheese dish, and cold appetizers such as scordalia ($4.50), a deliciously garlicky potato dip. The revithia ($2.75), a chickpea soup served only occasionally, is a must-try. Greek pasta dishes include the hilopita "agrotiki" ($10.95), linguine tossed with artichoke hearts, mushrooms, broccoli, and sun-dried tomatoes in a yogurt-fennel sauce. The mousakas nestisimos ($9.95), a meatless version of the classic Greek dish of layered eggplant, zucchini, potatoes, and cheese in a bechamel sauce, is serviceable but bland. The desserts, however, are phenomenal. The baklava ($2.95) is not too sweet and the bougatsa ($2.95), lemon custard wrapped in fillo leaves, is surprisingly light. The kombosta me yiaourti ($4.50) is a delightful mix of dried fruits in tangy yogurt with just a touch of cinnamon and brown sugar. Best bet: come in the summer when you can dine on the rooftop, order a couple of appetizers, and move straight on to dessert.

FULL MENU WITH MANY VEGETARIAN OFFERINGS

★★ / $$$
21. Pili Pili

230 West Kinzie Street
Chicago IL 60610
312.464.9988
www.pilipilirestaurant.com

FRENCH

Hours:	Mon-Th 11:30 a.m. to 10:00 p.m.
	(cafe menu 2:00 p.m. to 5:30 p.m.)
	Fri 11:30 a.m. to 11:00 p.m.
	(cafe menu 2:00 p.m. to 5:30 p.m.)
	Sat 5:30 p.m. to 11:00 p.m.
	Sun 5:00 p.m. to 10:00 p.m.
Payment:	Credit cards accepted
Parking:	Valet
Alcohol:	Full bar
Atmosphere:	Upscale

Because so much French food is a turn-off for vegetarians (think escargot, steak frites, and cassoulet), Pili Pili's main attraction for vegetarians is that there's something to eat. In truth, most of that comes from the chef's strong Mediterranean influence. The light, airy room is a pleasant place for a leisurely meal. Start with excellent flatbread delivered in small white bags. The beet salad is a winner ($8), as is the tarte tatin with artichoke, fennel, oven-dried tomatoes, and Parmesan cheese ($8). Other highlights include the goat cheese ravioli with spinach, tomatoes, and basil ($10.50), and the roasted sweet red pepper filled with goat cheese ($7.50), but the hands-down favorite is the chickpea and cumin fries ($5.50). Skip the minestrone soup, which is nothing out of the ordinary.

FULL MENU WITH SOME VEGETARIAN OPTIONS

★★ / $$
22. Privata

> 935 North Damen Avenue
> Chicago, IL 60622
> 773.727.5292
>
> **ITALIAN/MEXICAN**
>
> | | |
> |---|---|
> | *Hours:* | Mon-Th 5:00 p.m. to 10:30 p.m. |
> | | Fri-Sat 5:00 p.m. to 11:30 p.m. |
> | | Sun 5:00 p.m. to 9:00 p.m. |
> | *Payment:* | Credit cards accepted |
> | *Parking:* | Street parking available |
> | *Alcohol:* | BYO, corkage fee 50 cents per person |
> | *Atmosphere:* | European-style cafe, with adjacent art gallery |

Those who remember Privata from one of its previous locations on Chicago Avenue may be surprised at how the restaurant has been spruced up. Gone are the white papers and pencils on each table encouraging doodling, and gone are the doodles of previous diners on the walls and ceilings. The new Privata also has a more scaled-back menu with fewer options, albeit just as good. Most of the Italian/Mexican hybrid menu can easily be made vegetarian, and you can watch Mario Rios, Privata's chef, make your orders in the small, open kitchen. You pair the pasta of your choice ($12) with one of his signature sauces, all made without meat stock. The chipotle black bean pesto, the avocado cream, and the mole verdi pesto are all good examples of the Italian/Mexican hybrid tastes hard to find elsewhere. The Mexicali raviolis ($6) change daily. Be sure to order if they're stuffed with mushroom on the day you visit. The spicy grilled veggie or roasted corn and black bean soups ($4.75) are also wise choices. Portions are large, even if the menu is not.

FULL MENU WITH MANY VEGETARIAN OFFERINGS

★★ / $$
23. Reza's

432 West Ontario Street
Chicago, IL 60610
312.664.4500

MEDITERRANEAN

Hours: Daily 11:00 a.m. to midnight
Payment: Credit cards accepted
Parking: Street parking can be difficult
Alcohol: Full bar
Atmosphere: Midscale, family-friendly

Other locations:
See North Side on page 69

For vegetarians and carnivores alike, the large menu and large portions at Reza's are legendary. In fact, Reza's is rather legendary as a place that is accessible to Middle Eastern–cuisine neophytes, but authentic enough to attract those who know their hummus from their baba ghanooj. A couple of appetizers are enough for a full meal; an entrée will definitely leave you with leftovers for lunch the next day. Among the items not to miss are the Persian Grilled Potatoes marinated in a house dressing ($3.50), a house specialty cooked just enough to be thoroughly done but not mushy. Also try the Dolmeh Felfel ($3.95), a baked sweet pepper, and the Vegetarian Shami ($3.95), with a pomegranate sauce. The big portions make Reza's a good choice for dining out with a crowd. Food quality doesn't suffer with Reza's excellent delivery service.

FULL MENU WITH MANY VEGETARIAN OFFERINGS

★★★ / $$
24. Russian Tea Time

77 East Adams Street
Chicago, IL 60603
312.360.0000
www.russianteatime.com

RUSSIAN

Hours:	*Sun-Mon 11:00 a.m. to 9:00 p.m.*
	Tue-Th 11:00 a.m. to 11:00 p.m.
	Fri-Sat 11:00 a.m. to midnight
	Summer hours vary; call ahead
Payment:	*Credit cards accepted*
Parking:	*Pay lots nearby at underground Grant Park parking garage, self-park garage across the street*
Alcohol:	*Full bar, with "famous vodka shots"*
Atmosphere:	*More old-world gentleman's club than tearoom*

Vegetarian-friendly cuisine from Uzbekistan is not an oxymoron—at least not at Russian Tea Time. A good portion of the large Slavic menu is vegetarian, so much so that even meat-eaters order from these pages. The pumpkin-filled vareniky (five for $7.95) are irresistibly topped with cinnamon butter, as is the Kiev cabbage-apple salad ($3.95). Several vegetarian platters, with samples of many of the menu items, are available for $38 (or $52 for three people), and may be the best way to try the different stews (mung bean and domlama, the layered vegetable stew) without overindulging. Of course, indulging is part of the culture at Russian Tea Time. Be sure to try both the platter of pastries ($5.95) and some of the "famous vodka shots." House vodka flavors include tea, coriander, caraway, horseradish, ginger, peppermint, lime, pineapple, pepper, coffee, and cinnamon.

FULL MENU WITH MANY VEGETARIAN AND VEGAN OFFERINGS

★★ / $
25. Salad Spinners

200 West Monroe Street (enter on Wells Street)
Chicago, IL 60606
312.269.5300
www.saladspinners.com

AMERICAN

Hours: Mon-Fri 7:00 a.m. to 3:00 p.m.
Payment: Credit cards accepted
Parking: Metered parking, pay lots
Alcohol: No
Atmosphere: Healthy fast-food take-out chain

Other locations:
AON Center, 200 East Randolph Street
   (lower level), Chicago, IL 60601, 312.861.1740
318 West Randolph Street, Chicago, IL 60601
   312.795.9555

The main attraction at this fresh fast-food chain is the menu of ten vegetarian salads that can be customized by request ($4.95 to $5.29). Many choices are traditional, like the Little Italy (with roasted red peppers, tortellini, and romaine lettuce in an Italian vinaigrette) or the Greek Islands salad (with tomatoes, cucumbers, kalamata olives, feta cheese, and dill dressing). Others veer off into more distinctive territory, like the suitably seasoned Mexicali (with corn, black beans, tortilla strips, and a spicy peanut sauce) or the sweet Tropical Sunsplash (with mangoes, oranges, and strawberries in a honey poppyseed dressing). Or, pick up a pencil and fill out the "dream card" to completely customize a salad from a list of more than fifty ingredients (not counting additional nonvegetarian toppings; each topping varies between $.35 and $2.19). Soups change daily, but a popular vegetarian butternut squash soup is available every day ($3.29). Sandwiches are available but strictly for carnivores.

MANY VEGETARIAN OFFERINGS

★★★ / $$
26. Sangria Restaurant and Tapas Bar

>   901 West Weed Street
>   Chicago, IL 60622
>   312.266.1200

SPANISH

Hours:	*Mon-Th 5:00 p.m. to 10:00 p.m.*
	Fri 5:00 p.m. to midnight
	Sat 11:00 a.m. to midnight
	Sun 11:00 a.m. to 10:00 p.m.
Payment:	*Credit cards accepted*
Parking:	*Valet ($2)*
Alcohol:	*Full bar with six kinds of sangria*
Atmosphere:	*Late-night twenty-something scene*

In the old Bub City location, Sangria Restaurant and Tapas Bar has all the trappings of a Lincoln Park stereotype: 6,000 square feet of loud music, a twenty-something crowd, and a late-night liquor license. But Sangria transcends all that with two pleasant surprises: good food and attentive service. The staff knows its large menu and is able to answer questions about which oils and condiments are used with which dishes. Vegetarian menu items are marked with a V, and at press time the kitchen was working on retooling some recipes to make even more of the menu veg-friendly. In addition to the standard veg-friendly tapas, such as tortilla Espanola ($3.50) and garlic potato salad ($3.50), there's the much harder to find vegetarian paella ($10.50). Skip the average sliced olives, which don't meet the quality and presentation standards of the other tapas. Of course, you'd be remiss if you didn't order one of the six kinds of sangria on the menu. The cava (Spanish champagne) version is cause to celebrate.

FULL MENU WITH MANY VEGETARIAN AND VEGAN OFFERINGS

★★ / $$
27. Sayat Nova

157 East Ohio Street
Chicago, IL 60611
312.644.9159

ARMENIAN

Hours:	Mon-Sat 11:30 a.m. to 10:30 p.m.
	Sun 3:00 p.m. to 10:00 p.m.
Payment:	Credit cards accepted
Parking:	Validated pay lot
Alcohol:	Full bar
Atmosphere:	Family-owned grotto

For more than thirty-five years Sayat Nova has been a rarity off the Magnificent Mile: a reasonably priced, non-chain restaurant. Yep, this family-owned Armenian spot serves up couscous, stuffed grape leaves, and other Middle Eastern delights with the best of them. Diners are greeted with a big basket of pita bread for the table. Evenings, with live music and hookah smoking in the cave-like space, tend to get loud and smoky, which doesn't make Sayat Nova a good choice for a quiet night, but the private booths make a clandestine date night a possibility. The waitstaff is attentive and polite, another rarity at affordable downtown dining establishments.

FULL MENU WITH MANY VEGETARIAN OFFERINGS

★ / $
28. Star of Siam

11 East Illinois Street
Chicago, IL 60611
312.670.0100

THAI

Hours:	*Sun-Th 10:00 a.m. to 9:30 p.m.*
	Fri-Sat 10:00 a.m. to 10:30 p.m.
Payment:	*Credit cards accepted*
Parking:	*Street parking difficult, valet*
Alcohol:	*Full bar*
Atmosphere:	*Midscale, business-friendly restaurant*

This bustling River North restaurant is a favorite for good, fresh Thai food. Lofty, wood-beamed ceilings and large windows create an airy feel, and dazzling Thai costumes adorn the walls. Traditional sunken tables with patterned pillows for seats offer a cozy change of pace; though tricky to maneuver in and out of, they're surprisingly comfortable. Salads, vegetable stir-fries, and rice and noodle dishes provide plenty of vegetarian and some vegan choices. Fried tofu is a surprisingly light but bland starter. Instead, try poh-pia sod, a delicate spring roll wrap of bean sprouts, cucumber, cooked tofu, and scrambled eggs. In the rama tofu (substituting for chicken), deliciously kicky peanut sauce flavors stir-fried tofu and perfectly steamed broccoli. Pad see eiw with pillowy tofu mixes browned wide rice noodles and a mildly spicy sauce. Friendly Thai servers are happy to substitute tofu for meat or fish entrées, but curry dishes have a fish-sauce base. Entrées $5.95 to $7.25.

FULL MENU WITH MANY VEGETARIAN AND VEGAN OPTIONS

★★★★ / $$$
29. Tizi Melloul

531 North Wells Street
Chicago, IL 60610
312.670.4338

MEDITERRANEAN

Hours:	Mon-Wed 5:30 p.m. to 10:00 p.m.
	Th 5:00 p.m. to 10:00 p.m.
	Fri-Sat 5:00 p.m. to 11:00 p.m.
	Sun 5:00 p.m. to 10:00 p.m.
Payment:	Credit cards accepted
Parking:	Valet ($10)
Alcohol:	Full bar
Atmosphere:	Intimate Moroccan theme

In less-accomplished hands, Tizi Melloul could come off as Disney-esque: flamenco guitar nights, belly dancers, alcohol shots with fried sweet potato flakes, floor seating, and hookah pipes. But instead of kitsch, Tizi Melloul is that rare combination of fun and high-quality food. Like most restaurants with serious chefs at the helm, the menu changes, based on what's available seasonally. Tempting veg-friendly options include the mezze salad of baba ghanooj, tapenade, and tabbouleh ($7); the griddled polenta cake, Summer Vegetable Escalivida, goat cheese gelato, with spiced tomato water ($17); and Israeli couscous, dried fruit, and pine nuts ($5). For those who are less hungry—or on a tighter budget—there's a smaller tapas menu available at the bar. For those with more time and cash, a $30 prix fixe dinner is available in the Crescent Room, the sit-on-the-floor private room where eating with your hands is recommended.

FULL MENU WITH MANY VEGETARIAN OFFERINGS

★★★ / $
30. Tokyo Lunchbox

179 West VanBuren Street
Chicago, IL 60605
312.435.4006

JAPANESE

Hours: Mon-Fri 6:00 a.m. to 6:00 p.m.
Payment: Credit cards accepted
Parking: Street
Alcohol: No
Atmosphere: Fast food

Other locations:
111 East Wacker Drive, Chicago, IL 60601
   312.938.4450
37 North Wells Street, Chicago, IL 60606
   312.551.0797
222 Merchandise Mart, Chicago, IL 60654
   312.222.0690

Although not exclusively vegetarian, Tokyo Lunchbox draws non-meat eaters from all over downtown who come to sample veggie maki rolls, like avocado with asparagus, shiitake mushroom, oshinko (Japanese pickled radish), cucumber, and others ($3.50 to $4.99). Dumplings are a particular favorite, including vegetable gyoza and unusual edamame-stuffed shumai. Other appetizers include gomae (spinach with sesame sauce), vegetable rice soup, miso soup, and a spicy tofu soup ($1.50 to $3.50). For a meal-sized soup, try udon noodle made with a vegetarian broth rarely found in Japanese restaurants and served with vegetables or veggie tempura. The veggie tempura is also available in an entrée size, as is teriyaki tofu served with steamed rice ($4.99). Finish up with green tea ice cream.

FULL MENU WITH MANY VEGETARIAN OFFERINGS

★★★★ / $$$
31. Vermilion

10 West Hubbard Street
Chicago, IL 60610
312.527.4060

INDIAN/LATIN AMERICAN

Hours:	Mon-Fri 11:30 a.m. to 2:30 p.m.
	5:00 p.m. to 10:00 p.m.
	Sat 5:00 p.m. to 11:00 p.m.
	Sun 5:00 p.m. to 10:00 p.m.
Payment:	Credit cards accepted
Parking:	Valet
Alcohol:	Full bar, open daily until approximately 2:00 a.m.
Atmosphere:	Upscale gathering place and bar

Indian/Latin American—it sounds weird, but in her effort as a restaurateur (she previously worked as a management consultant), Rohini Dey and her chef, Maneet Chauhan, have combined the flavors of these cuisines with similar climates in ways that complement rather than clash. The emphasis here is on tapas-like small plates that can be shared, making it a good spot for a light meal or for trying to introduce some vegetarian dishes to carnivores (not to mention a night out with a big group of friends). Almost everything on the menu is exceptionally presented and flavorful. Standouts include empanadas made with spinach-queso served with mango coconut chutney ($8), and the bharwa baingan baby eggplants stuffed and roasted with Indian spices and served with fresh parantha ($12). Save room for a yogurt shake of the day and desserts. Order the Chai Spice Cake ($8), with chai-flavored tres leches and a pear, ginger, and saffron chutney, it is unlike any you've sampled before.

FULL MENU WITH MANY VEGETARIAN OFFERINGS

★★★★ / $$$
32. Zealous

419 West Superior Street
Chicago, IL 60610
312.475.9112
www.zealousrestaurant.com

AMERICAN

Hours:	Tue-Sat 5:00 p.m. to 10:00 p.m. Closed Sun-Mon
Payment:	Credit cards accepted
Parking:	Easy street parking weeknights, use the valet weekends
Alcohol:	Full bar, many specialty drinks
Atmosphere:	Contemporary

Since he moved Zealous from suburban Elmhurst to the crowded River North neighborhood, chef/owner Michael Taus has been doing the unexpected. His minimalist 150-seat restaurant continues to do the same, starting with the vegetarian friendliness of its menu. Taus estimates that 20 percent of his high-end clientele are vegetarians. On any given day, the menu, which changes based on seasonal availability, includes a large number of vegetarian creations, such as the roasted eggplant gateau with golden tomato coulis ($15) and a house-made ravioli with Manchego cheese, baby carrots, and asparagus ($18). Taus enjoys the artistry of the kitchen, and as a result he'll make special vegan and vegetarian multicourse meals on request. One vegetarian regular, he says, has never been served the same dish twice, and has dined at Zealous more than 200 times. Lucky man.

FULL MENU WITH MANY VEGETARIAN AND VEGAN OFFERINGS

South Side

★★ / $$
1. Cedars Mediterranean Kitchen

1206 East 53rd Street
Chicago, IL 60615
773.324.6227

MEDITERRANEAN

Hours:	Daily 11:30 a.m. to 10:00 p.m.
Payment:	Credit cards accepted
Parking:	Free lot
Alcohol:	BYO, no corkage fee
Atmosphere:	Middle Eastern meets Jetsons cafeteria

Cedars sits in Kimbark Plaza, one of Hyde Park's many nondescript strip malls. But its interior is neither what you'd expect for a strip mall nor is it a traditional Mediterranean restaurant. The decor is 1970s Space Age, with funky light fixtures, brightly colored walls, and an open kitchen. From that kitchen, start with the lentil soup ($2) or an amazing platter of red potato wedges ($2.95). Follow with the eggplant stew ($7.50) or the vegan tomato couscous ($8.95), and you won't have to eat for the rest of the day. Thanks to big portions, free parking, and good food close to campus, Cedars does a brisk take-out business from U of C types.

FULL MENU WITH MANY VEGETARIAN AND VEGAN OFFERINGS

★★ / $
2. El Faro

3936 West 31st Street
Chicago, IL 60623
773.277.1155

MEXICAN

Hours:	*Daily 5:00 a.m. to 11:00 p.m.*
Payment:	*Credit cards accepted*
Parking:	*Street parking possible, some surrounding streets require a permit*
Alcohol:	*No*
Atmosphere:	*Family-friendly cafeteria*

More so than in many Pilsen restaurants, El Faro ("The Lighthouse") is almost entirely Spanish-language, from its menu to its servers. If Spanish is not your native tongue and you don't remember your high school language coursework, you still should not shy away from a try at this vegetarian- and vegan-friendly restaurant. Servers are polite and will tolerate pointing for the linguistically challenged. Point your index finger to any variety of fresh fruit juices and blends, such as grapes, lime, and pineapple. Don't pass up the tofu scramble, a spicy blend with eggs and beans. You'll want to cool down your mouth with the soft tortillas (not chips) that are brought to the table (counter service and takeout also available). If you're hungry, you might break a $10 bill.

FULL MENU WITH MANY VEGETARIAN AND VEGAN OFFERINGS

★ / $
3. Ex Libris Coffee Shop

The Joseph Regenstein Library, Room A021
1100 East 57th Street
Chicago, IL 60637
773.702.7645
exlibris.uchicago.edu

MULTIETHNIC

Hours:	Mon-Th 8:30 a.m. to 11:30 p.m.
	Fri 8:30 a.m. to 5:00 p.m.
	Sun 2:00 p.m. to 11:30 p.m.
	Closed Sat (call for summer hours)
Payment:	Cash only
Parking:	Street parking can be difficult
Alcohol:	No
Atmosphere:	Campus coffee shop

This student-run coffee shop inside the Joseph Regenstein Library on the University of Chicago campus has exactly the vibe you'd expect of a student-run joint. That means hours based on school schedules, a what-do-you-want attitude from servers, and amazingly low prices. Without a kitchen of its own, Ex Libris gets its goods from local restaurants, including The Nile, Briazz, Pizza Capri, and Thai 55, among others. Meatless treats include yogurts, desserts, granola, cereal, and soups. Prices start at 25 cents for pita bread and rarely exceed $10. Ex Libris isn't worth a trip to Hyde Park, but if you're a student or visitor to U of C and need an affordable bite, it is one of the easiest choices on campus.

FULL MENU WITH MANY VEGETARIAN OFFERINGS

★★ / $
4. I.C.Y. Vegetarian Restaurant and Juice Bar

3141 West Roosevelt Road
Chicago, IL 60612
773.762.1090

MULTIETHNIC

Hours:	Mon-Sat 8:00 a.m. to 7:00 p.m. Closed Sun
Payment:	Credit cards accepted
Parking:	Ample street parking
Alcohol:	No
Atmosphere:	Neighborhood diner

Formerly called New Life Vegetarian Restaurant and Juice Bar, this Lawndale all-veg spot is more than just a juice bar. The tables (with stools), scarcely a handful, are decorated with flower vases to spruce things up and to clue you in that you're not in for standard-issue fare. Sure, there's the "Stakelet" ($2.69 for a lunch sandwich, $7.25 as part of the Tuesday dinner special) and the veggie burger ($2.69). But there are also unexpected entrées, including options on the breakfast menu (served until noon) such as veggie sausage, tofu eggs, and brown rice scallop potatoes, plus biscuits ($4.25). Save room for delicious desserts, including lemon icebox pie ($2.50) and sweet potato pie ($2.25).

VEGETARIAN WITH MANY VEGAN OFFERINGS

★★ / $$
5. Joy Yee's Noodle Shop

2159 South China Place
Chicago, IL 60616
312.328.0001
www.joyyee.com

PAN-ASIAN

Hours:	Mon-Sun 11:00 a.m. to 10:30 p.m.
Payment:	Credit cards accepted
Parking:	Metered street parking
Alcohol:	No
Atmosphere:	Bubble tea joint with a young and hip crowd

Other locations:
See Suburban Cook County on page 146

Chinatown has become a magnet for lovers of authentic Asian eats and bubble drinks (blended fruit drinks with balls of tapioca "bubbles"). While the food isn't as veg-friendly as it could be, the tropical fruit "freezes"—fresh fruit, ice, and syrup—bring vegans to the restaurant in droves. At $2.95 to $3.50 for a large portion, they're also a bargain. The indecisive have their work cut out: there are more than a hundred fruit choices and combinations (lychee, avocado, papaya, honeydew, and taro are some of the more unconventional), plus several drink varieties to choose from, including freeze, cream freeze, jelly (gummi-worm-like strips), and others. The staff happily accommodates off-menu smoothie requests (a peach and mango cream freeze is highly recommended). Prefer chewing to slurping? Tall cups of very fresh mixed fruit are $3.75. If you get a table close to the blender-roaring smoothie bar, the noise can be pretty loud. Patrons who just want to grab a smoothie and run can use the walk-up ordering window in the vestibule.

FULL MENU WITH SOME VEGETARIAN OFFERINGS

★★ / $$
6. Leona's

1236 East 53rd Street
Chicago, IL 60615
773.363.2600
www.leonas.com

ITALIAN

Hours:	Mon-Th 11:30 a.m. to 11:30 p.m.
	Fri 11:30 a.m. to 12:30 a.m.
	Sat noon to 12:30 a.m.
	Sun noon to 10:30 p.m.
Payment:	Credit cards accepted
Parking:	Free lot
Alcohol:	Full bar, including organic beer and wine
Atmosphere:	Family-friendly midscale

Other locations in South Side Chicago:
11060 South Western Avenue, 773.881.7700
7601 South Cicero Avenue, 773.838.8383
See also North Side on page 56; Downtown on page 99; Suburban Cook County on page 149

Leona's bills itself as a "closet vegetarian" joint with an emphasis on fresh, wholesome ingredients. So dig in with reassurance to the portobello and white mushrooms in whole wheat ravioli; a vegan burger made of tofu, sliced mushrooms, sunflower seeds, and rolled oats; and grilled flatbread wraps stuffed with tofu, roasted veggies, or hummus. The deep-dish pizza ($21.50 for a large) is made with a touch of cornmeal in the crust. Toppings include pesto or hummus instead of typical tomato sauce. Soy cheese is also available. Entrées range from $11 to $25 and pasta/sandwiches/burgers from $8.50 to $13.

FULL MENU WITH MANY VEGETARIAN AND VEGAN OFFERINGS

★★ / $$
7. Mellow Yellow

1508 East 53rd Street
Chicago, IL 60615
773.667.2000

AMERICAN

Hours:	Mon-Th 6:00 a.m. to 9:00 p.m.
	Fri-Sat 6:00 a.m. to 11:00 p.m.
	Sun 6:00 a.m. to 10:00 p.m.
Payment:	Credit cards accepted
Parking:	Metered street parking
Alcohol:	Full bar
Atmosphere:	Midscale

A Hyde Park institution since 1976, Mellow Yellow seems to add a page to its menu for every year it's in business. With its truly exhaustive menu, nearly everyone can find something they'll like. But a lot of visitors never get past the star attraction: award-winning vegetarian chili, available "one way" (chili only), "five-way" (chili over spaghetti with shredded cheese, onions, and sour cream), or any way in between ($4.50 to $5.95). Chili even puts in an appearance at breakfast, served with eggs. But for those less enamored of the bean, there is no shortage of other options. If Mellow Yellow has another specialty, it's the crepes, which are available in breakfast, dinner, and dessert variations, offering combinations ranging from mushroom and cheese and Florentine to hot fudge and banana brown sugar. A wide assortment of vegetarian-friendly pastas and salads are available ($6.25 to $9.95), as well as other 1970s-era standards like veggie quiche and stuffed baked potatoes.

FULL MENU WITH MANY VEGETARIAN OPTIONS

★ / $
8. A Natural Harvest

7122 South Jeffrey Avenue
Chicago, IL 60649
773.363.3939

MULTIETHNIC

Hours:	Mon-Fri 11:00 a.m. to 7:00 p.m.
	Sat 10:00 a.m. to 6:30 p.m.
	Closed Sun
Payment:	Credit cards accepted
Parking:	Street parking possible
Alcohol:	No
Atmosphere:	Grocery store deli

Tucked in the back of a natural foods and supplements store in South Shore, A Natural Harvest's deli counter offers a small variety of vegan salads and sandwiches ($2.50 to $6.50), as well as fresh juices and nutritional drinks ($1.65 to $9). Salads, sold by weight, include faux chicken, vegetable carrot tuna, and simpler offerings like the mixed raw salad. Sandwiches mostly lean towards meatless versions of classic cold cuts, such as veggie turkey, chicken, corned beef, and "Wham." Veggie hoagies, burgers, and "Stakelet" sandwiches round out the food menu. The juice bar offers carrot, mixed vegetable, and wheatgrass shots, as well as energy and protein drinks. The menu lists a number of soups that sound appetizing, though they're not always available. A few limited seats are on the premises.

MOSTLY VEGAN

★★ / $$
9. The Nile

1611 East 55th Street
Chicago, IL 60615
773.324.9499

MIDDLE EASTERN

Hours:	Mon-Sat 11:00 a.m. to 9:00 p.m.
	Sun noon to 8:00 p.m.
Payment:	Credit cards accepted
Parking:	Metered street parking
Alcohol:	No
Atmosphere:	Midscale

A favorite with the University of Chicago crowd, The Nile offers a conventional but high-quality variety of Middle Eastern delicacies. Besides a much-beloved lentil soup, other starters include hummus, baba ghanooj, spinach pie, and the slightly less common mashwiya (a puree of squash, yogurt, garlic, and mint; $1.50 to $1.95). Perhaps unsurprisingly, tasty falafel makes several appearances on the menu as an appetizer, a sandwich, and an entrée (just in case you forgot it was available). Vegetarian entrées include vegetable tagin, stuffed squash, and maklouba (mixed vegetables with rice and yogurt), and come with a choice of soup or one of four Middle Eastern salads ($8 to $9). And don't neglect to turn the page to look beyond the vegetarian section. Hidden within the "Middle Eastern Delights" portion of the menu are such gems as fattah (toasted bread and chickpea stock) and delicious foul (fava beans).

FULL MENU WITH MANY VEGETARIAN OPTIONS

★ / $$
10. Phoenix Restaurant and Phoenix Noodle and Dumpling House

2131 South Archer Avenue
Chicago, IL 60616
312.328.0848 / 312.328.1205

CHINESE

Hours:	*Restaurant:*
	Mon-Fri 9:00 a.m. to 10:00 p.m.
	Sat 8:00 a.m. to 11:00 p.m.
	Sun 8:00 a.m. to 10:00 p.m.
	Dumpling House:
	Mon, Wed-Th 11:00 a.m. to 10:00 p.m.
	Fri-Sat 11:00 a.m. to 11:00 p.m.
	Closed Tue
Payment:	*Credit cards accepted*
Parking:	*On the street or in lot one block east of the restaurant at Wentworth and Archer Avenues*
Alcohol:	*Yes*
Atmosphere:	*Upstairs banquet hall; downstairs hip snack bar*

Chinese food can be hard for vegetarians to negotiate, with its bits of meat and fish-based sauces. Dim sum dumplings can be almost impossible; you can't be sure what's inside until you take a bite. While Phoenix is not a standout, this duo is one of Chinatown's best for vegetarians, particularly those in search of dim sum. The steamed vegetarian dumplings ($4.95 for six) are tender. The lotus-seed pate buns ($2.45 for three) are glutinous with a sweet filling and studded with seeds. The vegetarian spring rolls ($2.50 for two) have a tasty filling of rice noodles and vegetables, but the crisp wrapper is too oily. In addition to desserts, other veggie picks include braised bean curd with Chinese mushroom ($10.95) and the moo shu vegetables, which do not appear on the menu.

FULL MENU WITH SOME VEGETARIAN OPTIONS

★★ / $
11. Rajun Cajun

1459 East 53rd Street
Chicago, IL 60615
773.955.1145

INDIAN AND SOUL FOOD

Hours:	Mon-Sat 11:00 a.m. to 10:00 p.m.
	Sun noon to 9:00 p.m.
Payment:	Credit cards accepted
Parking:	Street
Alcohol:	No
Atmosphere:	Fast food

Most people think Hyde Park doesn't have an Indian restaurant. That's probably because Hyde Park's Indian restaurant is called "Rajun Cajun." Often named by the student newspaper at the nearby University of Chicago as the best vegetarian option in the neighborhood, this small, quick-service restaurant offers an eclectic mix of Indian and soul food. On a typical day, the restaurant provides five to seven Indian dishes, the majority of which are vegetarian offerings like chana masala and sag paneer. Accompanying dishes include traditional Indian rice, samosas, and even mango lassi. On the soul-food side, most people come for the decidedly nonvegetarian fried chicken, but side items like greens and mac 'n' cheese are a big veggie draw. The best bargain to be had is one of the combination plates, which allows mixing and matching among the many options. (Usually people stick with the Indian or soul-food themes, but if you want black-eyed peas with your chai, go ahead and ask.) Entrées range from $7 to $10.

**FULL MENU WITH MANY
VEGETARIAN OFFERINGS**

★★ / $
12. Soul Vegetarian East

205 East 75th Street
Chicago, IL 60619
773.224.0104

SOUL FOOD

Hours:	Mon-Th 7:00 a.m. to 10:00 p.m.
	Fri-Sat 7:00 a.m. to 11:00 p.m.
	Sun 8:00 a.m. to 9:00 p.m.
Payment:	Credit cards accepted
Parking:	Easy street parking available
Alcohol:	No
Atmosphere:	Earnest midscale eatery

Soul Vegetarian East has a reputation that is much larger than its modest storefront. The vibe of this twenty-year-old-plus Chatham eatery is decidedly downscale. Faded pink walls are covered with posters of John Coltrane and Miles Davis, but the focus here is on the food. The no-animal-products menu features gluten and other protein substitutes to make tempting vegan versions of soul favorites. Daily specials offer the best deals for those who are hungry, with an entrée such as barbeque gluten plus cornbread, greens, and other sides for a fixed price. Other favorites include the gluten roasts and the garvey burgers. Skip the veggie gyro ($4), which is essentially a falafel sandwich. While most dishes are vegan, some sauces contain honey, so it is best to check with your server. Because there is nowhere else quite like Soul Vegetarian East in Chicago, the wait for a table or for carryout orders can be long. (Some takeout, plus packaged goods, is available from the adjacent Eternity Juice Bar and Deli.) Prices range from $4 to $10.

VEGAN MENU WITH SOME HONEY AND WHEY INGREDIENTS

★ / $
13. Southtown Health Foods

2100 West 95th Street
Chicago, IL 60643
773.233.1856

Juice bar

Hours:	Mon-Sat 9:30 a.m. to 5:30 p.m.
	Th 9:30 a.m. to 8:00 p.m.
	Closed Sun
Payment:	Credit cards accepted
Parking:	Ample front lot, plus metered street parking
Alcohol:	No
Atmosphere:	Grocery store with limited seating

An independent natural foods store with an impressive selection of to-go goods, Southtown Health Foods also has a more-than-serviceable juice bar. In the front counter you'll find all the basics: carrot and carrot-vegetable-mix juices, plus plenty of premade veggie wraps, salads, tabbouleh, hummus, and other lunch foods. There's limited seating, but the counter is intended for takeout. If the weather's nice, take advantage of Beverly's many nearby impressive parks, including Ridge Park, and pack a picnic from Southtown.

Full menu with many vegetarian offerings

★ / $
14. U.S. Cellular Field

333 West 35th Street
Chicago, Illinois 60616
312.674.1000
chicago.whitesox.mlb.com

BALLPARK EATS

Hours:	*During Chicago White Sox games*
Payment:	*Cash at all concession stands, credit cards accepted at some*
Parking:	*$16 per car in adjacent lots*
Alcohol:	*Of course; it is a baseball game*
Atmosphere:	*Ballpark concession stands*

At U.S. Cellular Field, concession stands serve up nontraditional versions of the traditional ballpark favorite foods, namely, veggie dogs and burgers. A Morningstar veggie dog goes for $3.25 and a Gardenburger will set you back $4. Dollar Dog Thursdays at "The Cell" does not, unfortunately, apply to the veggie dogs. The v-dogs can be rubbery and tasteless, but let's be, um, frank—you'll go for the baseball, not the food. Vendors offer several snack options for vegetarians, and even some for vegans. A slice of cheese pizza is $4.50. Treats like funnelcakes, pretzels, elephant ears, french fries, nachos, chips, churros, Sno Cones, cotton candy, popcorn, and even peanut butter and jelly sandwiches will run you between $2 and $4 and are available on both the upper and lower levels. A Mexican cantina stand on the 100 level offers jalapeno poppers, burritos, and quesadillas. But if your ticket is for the park's upper levels, you won't be able to access the lower level or its food stands. And if you yearn for peanuts and Cracker Jack, they can be yours for just $2.50 and $3.50, respectively.

FULL MENU WITH SOME VEGETARIAN AND VEGAN OPTIONS

★★ / $
15. Vegetarian Fun Foods Supreme

1702 East 87th Street
Chicago, IL 60617
773.734.6321

MULTIETHNIC

Hours:	Mon-Sat 10:00 a.m. to 9:00 p.m. Closed Sun and holidays
Payment:	Credit cards accepted
Parking:	Metered street parking
Alcohol:	No
Atmosphere:	Fast food

With its seven utilitarian booths, bright orange walls, and beach-shack-style menu board, this unassuming fast-food joint near South Shore doesn't look like anything special. But Vegetarian Fun Foods Supreme is as surprising as its name. The menu is almost wholly vegan, with options of soy cheese or dairy cheese, and baked goods with honey clearly marked. Almost all the budget take-out items are solid choices, but the veggie chicken submarine ($3.99) and the spinach pizza ($6.99), both created with homemade baked goods, are solid choices. Neither the black-eyed pea soup ($1.49 to $5.99) nor the honey lemonade ($1.49) are to be missed. But save room for the fresh daily desserts, like the lemon yellow cake ($2.29) and the honey oatmeal square ($1.79). Skip the taco supreme ($1.49)—the shell is soggy and the seasoning of the veggie meat indeterminate—as well as the "natural" potato chips (they're Jay's); otherwise you're sure to have fun with your food.

**MOSTLY VEGAN, WITH SOME HONEY
AND DAIRY INGREDIENTS**

Suburban Cook County

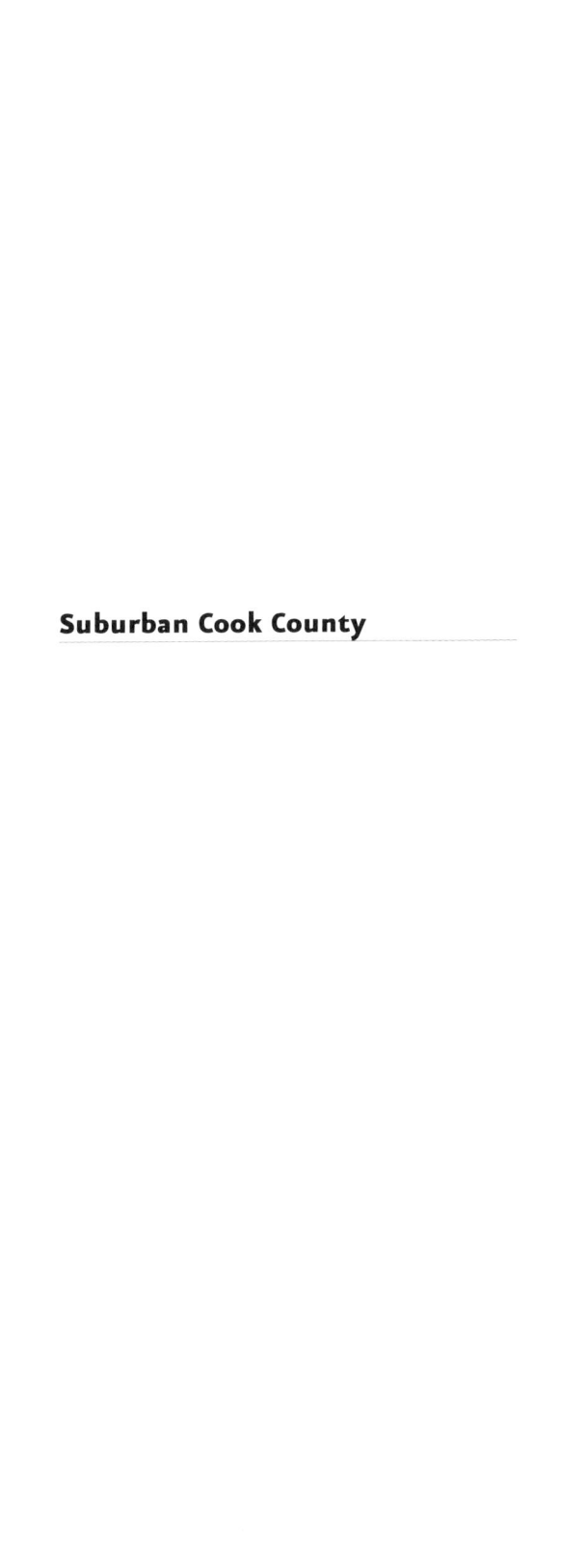

★★ / $$
1. A La Carte

111 Green Bay Road
Wilmette, IL 60091
847.256.4102
www.alacarteinc.com

MULTIETHNIC

Hours:	Mon-Fri 10:00 a.m. to 7:00 p.m.
	Sat 8:00 a.m. to 5:30 p.m.
	Closed Sun
Payment:	Credit cards accepted
Parking:	Small lot, street parking possible
Alcohol:	No
Atmosphere:	Gourmet grocery with takeout and seating

One of the North Shore's favorite take-out stops, A La Carte's menu changes weekly, with the current menu and the upcoming week's menu posted in the store and online. The majority of customers are here for to-go orders as fast-food alternatives or for picnics for concerts at nearby Ravinia and other summer events. The eat-in crowd, at small tables toward the front of the cozy store, includes ladies who lunch, retirees, and moms stopping in between shuttling kids to soccer practice and piano lessons. Vegetarian selections are clearly marked on the long menu and include such favorites as grilled asparagus, Spanish potato tortilla, red lentil soup, and spinach lemon pasta salad. Not-to-be-missed desserts include fruit cobblers and specialty bundt cakes. Most items are priced by the pound.

FULL MENU WITH MANY VEGETARIAN OFFERINGS

★★★ / $$
2. Blind Faith Cafe

525 Dempster Street
Evanston IL 60201
847.328.6875
www.blindfaithcafe.com

MULTIETHNIC

Hours: Mon-Fri 9:00 a.m. to 10:00 p.m.
Sat 8:00 a.m. to 10:00 p.m.
Sun 8:00 a.m. to 9:00 p.m.
Payment: Credit cards accepted
Parking: Metered street parking possible
Alcohol: No
Atmosphere: Eco-friendly midscale

One of the best-loved vegetarian restaurants in the Chicago area (the other being The Chicago Diner, page 32), Blind Faith is much more than its cafe name suggests. With seating in its pleasant dining room for more than a hundred, plus another thirty seats in the adjacent take-out bakery, Blind Faith is a hub of North Shore veg-friendliness. Unlike many restaurants with items like barbeque seitan sandwiches ($8.95) and macrobiotic plates ($11.25) on the menu, Blind Faith cares about presentation as well as taste and organic ingredients. Expect attractive arrangements of the popular corn and potato enchilada ($8.95), Korean bi bim bop ($10.25), and the rarer find of vegetarian paella ($11.95). Appetizers such as tofu satay ($7.25) and handmade Chinese pot stickers ($7.25) are sizeable enough for a mini meal, particularly if you want to save room for desserts from the on-site bakery. The flourless chocolate cake and peanut butter chocolate brownies are good bets, chased down with a cup of organic coffee.

VEGETARIAN WITH MANY VEGAN OFFERINGS

★★ / $$
3. Buzz Cafe

905 South Lombard Avenue
Oak Park, IL 60304
708.524.2899
www.thebuzzcafe.com

MULTIETHNIC

Hours:	Mon-Fri 6:00 a.m. to 9:00 p.m.
	Sat 7:00 a.m. to 9:00 p.m.
	Sun 8:00 a.m. to 2:00 p.m.
Payment:	Credit cards accepted
Parking:	Ample street parking
Alcohol:	No
Atmosphere:	Neighborhood coffee klatch

Buzz Cafe is Oak Park's Central Perk—that is, if the characters on *Friends* were community activists who gathered to discuss school reform. If you live in Oak Park, you're almost guaranteed to run into someone you know here. That's because of the welcoming, grown-up coffeehouse vibe and better-than-average coffee shop fare. Much of the menu is veg-friendly, including a section of vegetarian sandwiches such as grilled portobello ($5.50) and grilled garlic mushroom ($5.95) as well as an array of hearty appetizers. The Mediterranean potato pancakes ($4.50) are served with a garlic cucumber sauce, while the couscous salad ($4.50) is another filling meal option. Breakfast items are available with or without the traditional bacon or sausage. Organic eggs are available for an extra $1. The surrounding Harrison Street area is dotted with boutiques and locally owned businesses.

FULL MENU WITH MANY VEGETARIAN OFFERINGS

★★ / $$
4. The BUZZ

834 Lake Street
  (inside the Oak Park Public Library)
Oak Park, IL 60301
708.660.9500
www.thebuzzcafe.com

MULTIETHNIC

Hours:	Mon-Th 6:00 a.m. to 9:00 p.m.
	Fri 6:00 a.m. to 6:00 p.m.
	Sat 8:00 a.m. to 5:00 p.m.
	Sun 8:00 a.m. to 6:00 p.m.
Payment:	Credit cards accepted
Parking:	Ample street parking
Alcohol:	No
Atmosphere:	Take-out spin-off of popular coffee shop

Cafe Society, Buzz Cafe's weekly conversation group, moved to this Oak Park Library location spin-off, assuring that this mini version of the popular Buzz Cafe (see facing page) retains much of the original's vibe. The BUZZ menu is smaller than Buzz Cafe's but includes the veggie deluxe sandwich ($5.95) with cucumber and tomato, the hummus and pita platter ($3.50), as well as egg sandwiches, peanut butter and jelly sandwiches, and four salads. Like Buzz Cafe, the BUZZ has an ample kids' menu as well as juices, granitas, and baked goods.

FULL MENU WITH MANY VEGETARIAN OFFERINGS

★★ / $$
5. Chowpatti Vegetarian Restaurant

1035 South Arlington Heights Road
Arlington Heights, IL 60005
847.640.9554
www.chowpatti.com

MULTIETHNIC

Hours:	Tue-Sun 11:00 a.m. to 3:00 p.m.
	Tue-Th, Sun 5:00 p.m. to 9:00 p.m.
	Fri-Sat 5:00 p.m. to 10:00 p.m.
	Closed Mon
Payment:	Credit cards accepted
Parking:	Ample free lot
Alcohol:	No
Atmosphere:	Family-friendly casual

Chowpatti's 26-page menu is a virtual one-stop food court for vegetarians. Flipping through, you'll come across soups and salads, American favorites, northern and southern Indian cuisine, Italian dishes, Mexican plates, and Middle Eastern cuisine. Named after a beach in Bombay where street vendors sell a selection of different ethnic goods, Chowpatti makes decent, if not exceptional, versions of its multiethnic offerings. The vegetarian chili ($3.85) is flavorful and offered in a number of alternative presentations, such as in a pita, on nachos, in quesadillas, or on a veggie chili dog. From grilled-cheese sandwiches and pizzas ($4.25 to $11.75) to veggie lasagna ($7.95), the choices are solid. But as the smells inside this strip mall restaurant suggest, Indian food is the strength. Chowpatti offers more than fifteen curries, with daily specials, several varieties and sizes of bhaji (meatless stew), four kinds of uttapam, and more than a dozen kinds of dosai. A large list of fresh-squeezed juices allows you to quench your thirst after choosing your food at whatever spice levels you like. Service is polite and informative, if not speedy.

VEGETARIAN WITH MANY VEGAN OFFERINGS

★★ / $
6. Da'Nali's

4032 Oakton Street
Skokie, IL 60076
847.677.2782

MULTIETHNIC KOSHER/ITALIAN/AMERICAN

Hours:	Mon-Th 11:00 a.m. to 8:15 p.m.
	Sat 1 1/2 hours after sundown to 11:30 p.m.
	Sun noon to 8:15 p.m.
	Closed Fri
Payment:	Credit cards accepted
Parking:	Free shared lot
Alcohol:	BYO, no corkage fee
Atmosphere:	Family-friendly kosher pizza place

In an unassuming Skokie strip mall next to the Hungarian Kosher Foods supermarket (which shares an owner with Da'Nali's), this pizza place is easy to miss. But it is worth backtracking, as this is the only brick-oven, kosher vegetarian restaurant around. In a town that prides itself on pizza, Da'Nali's holds its own. The grilled veggie pizza features grilled seasonal vegetables, giving it a distinct flavor; the A.L.T. Sandwich has avocado and tomatoes. Pizza prices range from $7.50 to $13.95, plus charges for extra toppings. The interior is family-friendly, with high chairs, booster seats, and easy-to-wipe-clean tables. But the walls are adorned with Judaica art, making for a more cozy space than you'd expect. For dessert, brownies are rich and big enough to share. Like any good pizza place, Da'Nali's has take-out and delivery service.

MOSTLY VEGETARIAN; FISH ALSO SERVED

★★ / $
7. Fitness Cafe

70 South Arlington Heights Road
Arlington Heights, IL 60005
847.255.5799

MULTIETHNIC

Hours:	Mon-Sat 11:00 a.m. to 8:00 p.m. Closed Sun
Payment:	Credit cards accepted
Parking:	Free lot
Alcohol:	No
Atmosphere:	Fitness-themed cafe

Other locations:
See Collar Counties on page 162

Dining at Fitness Cafe can seem a bit like eating at the gym, minus the treadmills and sweaty guys in tank tops. But don't let the utilitarian atmosphere throw you—the food's delicious, and if you're watching your diet, you'll find plenty of options. The menu, posted on the wall, gives complete calorie counts for each item, as well as carbs, fat, and protein grams. Except for the low-carb menu, every food category—cold and hot sandwiches, wraps, pastas, kids' specials, and salads—has at least one vegetarian option. Sandwiches include the Free Style, layering grilled portobello mushrooms, cucumbers, avocados, tomatoes, red onions, and fresh organic greens, served with your choice of cheese on cracked whole wheat bread with special ranch dressing ($5.99 for a mere 355 calories). Or try the penne pasta with red and green peppers, diced portobello mushrooms, onions, and tomatoes ($5.99).

FULL MENU WITH VEGETARIAN OFFERINGS

★★ / $$
8. Flat Top Grill

726 Lake Street
Oak Park, IL 60301
708.358.8200

PAN-ASIAN

Hours:	Sun-Th 11:30 a.m. to 9:30 p.m.
	Fri-Sat 11:30 a.m. to 10:30 p.m.
Payment:	Credit cards accepted
Parking:	Street parking, valet on Fri and Sat after 5:00 p.m.
Alcohol:	Full bar
Atmosphere:	Friendly, midscale, make-your-own-meal chain

Other locations:
707 Church Street, Evanston, IL 60201
   847.570.0100
See also North Side on page 40; Downtown on page 89

This make-your-own stir-fry chain is a great place to take the whole brood. Grab a bowl from the stir-fry bar and fill it with your choice of rice, noodles, and fresh vegetables, then top it off with a few ladles from the selection of sauces (meat and fish eaters can also fill a side dish with beef, chicken, or seafood). Add a color-coded stick to turn your stir-fry into a wrap or soup, have it piled atop a bed of greens, or request it be cooked in a separate wok to avoid cross-contamination. The selection of ingredients changes quarterly to reflect local growing seasons. There's also a small menu of Asian-inspired appetizers, plus martinis and fruity tropical drinks. Unlimited trips to the stir-fry bar costs $7.99 at lunch and $12.99 at dinner for adults; meals for children ten and under are $4.99.

VEGETARIAN AND VEGAN OFFERINGS; MEAT, FISH, POULTRY, AND SEAFOOD ALSO SERVED

★ / $
9. Great American Bagel

6641 West Roosevelt Road
Berwyn, IL 60402
708.484.6611

MULTIETHNIC

Hours:	Mon-Fri 6:00 a.m. to 6:00 p.m.
	Sat-Sun 6:30 a.m. to 3:00 p.m.
Payment:	Credit cards accepted
Parking:	Free lot
Alcohol:	No
Atmosphere:	Take-out bagel shop

Fans of "real" New York–style bagels typically pass by outlets of this nondescript franchise, as do vegetarians who have no use for its specialty sandwiches with turkey and chicken. But at this one independently owned store of the 52-store chain, vegetarians are treated to a menu section of their own. Under the "Great American Garden" headline, you'll find hummus and vegetables, portobello mushroom sandwiches, garden burgers, and more—available for between $3.49 and $4.59, a price that includes a drink. Several salads and meat-free breakfast sandwiches are also available. Perfect for those who are in the Berwyn area (near Oak Park) and in need of a light meat-free snack.

CAFE MENU WITH VEGETARIAN OFFERINGS

★★ / $$
10. India House

> 228–230 McHenry Road
> Buffalo Grove, IL 60089
> 847.520.5569

INDIAN

Hours:	Mon-Fri 11:00 a.m. to 2:30 p.m.
	Sat-Sun 11:00 a.m. to 3:00 p.m.
	Sun-Th 5:00 p.m. to 10:00 p.m.
	Fri-Sat 5:00 p.m. to 11:00 p.m.
Payment:	Credit cards accepted
Parking:	Free mall lot
Alcohol:	Full bar
Atmosphere:	Family-friendly midscale

Other locations:
1473–1521 Schaumburg Road, Schaumburg, IL 60194, 847.895.5501
See also Downtown on page 96

India House, which caters to the suburban diner, is a spacious restaurant with a full bar and a raised dining area. While not lavish, the restaurant is a step up from many area eateries, with a staff more attentive than most. The large menu contains pages of both meat and vegetarian fare, and vegetable specialties are clearly marked. The aloo paratha ($4) disappoints traditionalists, as the potato is "baked in with the spices" instead of the more standard stuffed bread. Otherwise, dishes, including tandoori vegetables ($10.95), chili pakora ($4), and dal makhani ($11.95), meet expectations and are served to requested spice level. Try something off of the "Chaupati Corner" menu, which features "Bombay Street Fare." A children's menu has portions of the milder Indian foods as well as American foods for those whose young ones aren't as adventuresome.

FULL MENU WITH MANY VEGETARIAN AND VEGAN OFFERINGS

★★ / $$
11. Joy Yee's Noodle Shop

521 Davis Street
Evanston, IL 60201
847.733.1900
www.joyyee.com

PAN-ASIAN

Hours:	Mon-Th 11:30 a.m. to 10:00 p.m.
	Fri-Sat 11:30 a.m. to 10:30 p.m.
	Sun noon to 10:00 p.m.
Payment:	Credit cards accepted
Parking:	Metered street parking
Alcohol:	No
Atmosphere:	Bubble tea joint with a young and hip crowd

Other locations:
See South Side on page 124

This North Shore import from Chinatown has become a magnet for lovers of authentic Asian eats and bubble drinks (blended fruit drinks with balls of tapioca "bubbles"). While the food isn't as veg-friendly as it could be, the tropical fruit "freezes"—fresh fruit, ice, and syrup—bring vegans to the restaurant in droves. At $2.95 to $3.50 for a large portion, they're also a bargain. The indecisive have their work cut out: there are more than a hundred fruit choices and combinations (lychee, avocado, papaya, honeydew, and taro are some of the more unconventional), plus several drink varieties to choose from, including freeze, cream freeze, jelly (gummi-worm-like strips), and others. The staff happily accommodates off-menu smoothie requests (a peach and mango cream freeze is highly recommended). Prefer chewing to slurping? Tall cups of very fresh mixed fruit are $3.75.

FULL MENU WITH SOME VEGETARIAN OFFERINGS

★★ / $$
12. Kabul House

3320 West Dempster Avenue
Skokie, IL 60076
847.763.9930

AFGHAN

Hours:	Tue-Sat noon to 10:00 p.m.
	Sun-Mon 4:00 p.m. to 9:00 p.m.
Payment:	Credit cards accepted
Parking:	Small free lot
Alcohol:	BYO, no corkage fee
Atmosphere:	Nondescript casual

Other locations:
See North Side on page 52

Nestled in one of Dempster Avenue's many strip malls, Kabul House's Afghan-take on Middle Eastern favorites results in a sweeter hybrid of Persian and Indian delights. The must-try entrée is the Kadu Chalau ($8.95), a sautéed pumpkin dish with yogurt and mint. Another strong contender is the Sabzi Chalau ($8.95), sautéed spinach over basmati rice. Several of the rice dishes come with carrots and raisins to sweeten the pot. An appetizer of dal ($4.25) brings the flavors of India's seasoned lentils. Pita bread arrives thicker than standard, and is replenished by an attentive waitstaff.

**FULL MENU WITH MANY
VEGETARIAN OFFERINGS**

★★★ / $$
13. Khyber Pass

1031 Lake Street
Oak Park, IL 60301
708.445.9032

INDIAN

Hours:	*Daily 11:30 a.m. to 3:30 p.m.*
	5:00 p.m. to 10:00 p.m.
Payment:	*Credit cards accepted*
Parking:	*Several parking lots within one block*
Alcohol:	*Wine and beer*
Atmosphere:	*Upscale*

This popular Oak Park restaurant features a hot buffet with numerous vegetarian dishes as well as an a la carte menu with an ample section of vegetarian and vegan dishes. Vegetable oil is used with a light hand instead of ghee (clarified butter) in nearly all dishes. The mulligatawny soup and vegetable salfrazi (vegetables cooked with cheese in a spicy sauce) are flavorful, and the sag paneer is surprisingly light. Don't miss the bhel (puffed rice with potatoes and onions in an intriguing sauce) and the Khyber naan stuffed with onions, cheese, and potatoes and topped with poppy and sesame seeds, but skip the disappointing tandoori sabzi (vegetables roasted in the tandoor, which can be soggy and bland). The Indian waitstaff knows what vegan means and can steer you away from dishes containing cheese and from breads containing milk (naan) toward the ones that don't (poori and roti). Belly dancers perform on Saturday evenings and sitar musicians on some Friday evenings; other times, Indian music and the clatter of silverware fill the two rooms.

FULL MENU WITH MANY VEGETARIAN AND VEGAN DISHES

★★ / $$
14. Leona's

1455 Ring Road
Calumet City, IL 60409
708.868.4647
www.leonas.com

ITALIAN

Hours:	Mon-Th 11:00 a.m. to 1:00 p.m.
	Fri-Sat 11:00 a.m. to midnight
	Sun noon to 10:30 p.m.
Payment:	Credit cards accepted
Parking:	Free lot
Alcohol:	Full bar, including organic beer and wine
Atmosphere:	Family-friendly midscale

Other locations:
1504 Miner Street, Des Plaines, 847.759.0800
4431 West Roosevelt Road, Hillside, 708.449.0101
17501 Dixie Highway, Homewood, 708.922.9200
6616 West 95th Street, Oak Lawn, 708.430.7070
848 West Madison Street, Oak Park, 708.445.0101
43 West Dundee Road, Wheeling, 847.229.8080
See also North Side on page 56; Downtown on page 99; South Side on page 125

Leona's bills itself as a "closet vegetarian" joint with an emphasis on fresh, wholesome ingredients. So dig in with reassurance to the portobello and white mushrooms in whole wheat ravioli; vegan burger made of tofu, sliced mushrooms, sunflower seeds, and rolled oats; and grilled flatbread wraps stuffed with tofu, roasted veggies, or hummus. The deep-dish pizza ($21.50 for a large) reigns supreme, and is made with a touch of cornmeal in the crust. Toppings include pesto or hummus instead of typical tomato sauce. Soy cheese is also available. Entrées range from $11 to $25 and pasta/sandwiches/burgers from $8.50 to $13.

FULL MENU WITH MANY VEGETARIAN AND VEGAN OFFERINGS

★★ / $$
15. Little Egypt

7216 West College Drive
Palos Heights, IL 60463
708.923.0392

MEDITERRANEAN

Hours:	Sun-Th 11:00 a.m. to 9:00 p.m.
	Fri-Sat 11:00 a.m. to 2:00 a.m.
Payment:	Credit cards accepted
Parking:	Free lot
Alcohol:	Beer and wine
Atmosphere:	Strip mall oasis

A vibrant, fun Egyptian diversion in an otherwise unremarkable Palos Heights strip mall, Little Egypt is home to belly dancing, hookah pipes, and Middle Eastern music videos. Depending on the time of day, you may encounter large groups of friends enjoying a leisurely lunch or a more nightclub-like atmosphere. In addition to the social attraction of Little Egypt, its menu is a draw for south suburban vegetarians with limited eat-out options. The menu consists of dishes that are slight twists on the more familiar Persian and other Middle Eastern dishes. Among the favorites are attush, a salad with tomato, cucumber, and parsley baba ghanooj that has a slightly smoky flavor (maybe from the hookah smoke?). Portions are large; service can be slow. While you're waiting for your check, savor your katafi, an impressive Egyptian baklava. Prices from $3 to $14.

FULL MENU WITH MANY VEGETARIAN OFFERINGS; HONEY USED LIBERALLY

★★ / $$
16. Mt. Everest Restaurant

618 Church Street
Evanston, IL 60201
847.491.1069

INDIAN/NEPALI

Hours:	Mon-Fri 11:30 a.m. to 2:30 p.m.
	Sat-Sun noon to 3:00 p.m.
	Sun-Th 5:30 p.m. to 10:00 p.m.
	Fri-Sat 5:30 p.m. to 10:30 p.m.
Payment:	Credit cards accepted
Parking:	Street parking can be challenging, several nearby pay lots
Alcohol:	Beer and wine
Atmosphere:	Cozy midscale

No satisfying South Asian meal is complete without airy naan to mop up gravy and a cold mango lassi to balance spicy foods, and Mt. Everest Restaurant has both. The menu boasts both Indian and Nepali cuisine, which are listed separately. Mt. Everest offers twelve Indian vegetarian standards, like mutter paneer (creamed spinach with plentiful soft squares of white cheese), and chana masala (chickpeas in a spicy tomato- and onion-based gravy). The Nepali menu is slightly shorter and clearly lists ingredients, though some of the "mountain spices" may not be familiar to the average diner. All but two of the Nepali dishes are vegetarian, though most entrées, Indian and Nepali, contain ghee (clarified butter). Appetizers and accompaniments abound, from traditional vegetarian samosas to aloo paratha (thin bread stuffed with spiced mashed potatoes, then pan-fried). Entrée prices range from $6.95 to $13.95 for a vegetarian sampler plate, or thali, that includes dessert.

FULL MENU WITH MANY VEGETARIAN OFFERINGS

★★ / $
17. Noodles and Company

930 Church Street
Evanston, IL 60201
847.733.1200
www.noodles.com

MULTIETHNIC

Hours: Sun-Wed 11:00 a.m. to 9:00 p.m.
Th-Sat 11:00 a.m. to 10:00 p.m.
Payment: Credit cards accepted
Parking: Pay lot nearby
Alcohol: Beer and wine
Atmosphere: Midscale chain

Other locations:
20530 North Rand Road, Suite 201, Deer Park, IL 60010, 847.726.1000
66 South Arlington Heights Road, Arlington Heights, IL 60005, 847.577.1500
1851 Tower Drive, Glenview, IL 60025, 847.729.5555
1 East Burlington Avenue, La Grange, IL 60525, 708.579.1100
14662 La Grange Road, Unit B-1, Orland Park, IL 60462, 708.403.4400
See also Collar Counties on page 166

Italian, Japanese, Thai, and other cuisines are represented here, all by dishes with noodles as a primary ingredient. The Wisconsin mac 'n' cheese ($3.70 or $4.95) has fans who choose it over homemade. The Japanese pan noodles ($5.50) and the Indonesian peanut sauté ($5.75) both have strong flavors and are served in ample portions. If you aren't happy with your choice, a staff member happily brings you another entrée at no charge. While you order at the counter, your dishes are served to you at your table.

MOSTLY VEGETARIAN; CHICKEN, MEAT, AND FISH ALSO SERVED

★★★ / $$
18. PapaSpiros Greek Taverna

> 733 Lake Street
> Oak Park, IL 60302
> 708.358.1700

GREEK

> | | |
> |---|---|
> | Hours: | Mon-Th 11:00 a.m. to 11:00 p.m. |
> | | Fri-Sat 11:00 a.m. to midnight |
> | | Sun noon to 10:00 p.m. |
> | Payment: | Credit cards accepted |
> | Parking: | Street or in nearby lot |
> | Alcohol: | Full bar |
> | Atmosphere: | Comfortable casual |

This authentic Greek restaurant is far more veg-friendly than its counterparts in Chicago's Greektown. The servers helpfully steer diners to meatless dishes, such as the wonderful spanaki ($4.50), a generous side dish of lightly seasoned fresh spinach and rice. Don't miss the briami ($3.95), consisting of roasted eggplant, zucchini, carrot, pepper, onion, and potato in an herbed tomato sauce, or the Melitanosalata ($5.45), a roasted eggplant spread. The Fasolia Gigantes ($3.95) may end your aversion to lima beans. The Agginares Pasta ($11.95), a linguini dish with baby artichokes and fresh spinach in a lemon-garlic cream sauce, is addictive, and the vegetarian moussaka ($9.95) is light and delicious. If you're overwhelmed, try the Vegetarian Plate ($9.95), which includes small portions of spanakopita (spinach, feta, and herbs in phyllo leaves), briami, rice, oven-roasted potatoes, and green beans. Ordering family style is a good deal. For $19.95 per person (four-person minimum), you get to choose two appetizers, one salad, two main dishes, two sides, and two desserts.

FULL MENU WITH MANY VEGETARIAN OPTIONS

★★ / $$
19. Slice of Life

    4120 West Dempster Avenue
    Skokie, IL 60076
    847.674.2021

MULTIETHNIC KOSHER

Hours:	Mon-Th 11:30 a.m. to 9:00 p.m.
	Fri 11:30 a.m. to 3:00 p.m. (2:00 p.m. in winter)
	Sat $1/2$ hour after dark to 1:00 a.m.
	Sun 9:00 a.m. to 9:00 p.m.
Payment:	Cash and check only
Parking:	Free lot to the east (do not use the one to the west or you will be towed)
Alcohol:	Full bar
Atmosphere:	Quiet casual

Slice of Life is a friendly, inviting eatery on the North Shore. Order a drink from the full bar and select from a wide range of veg-friendly and nondairy menu items not often found on vegetarian menus. For example, the kosher kitchen serves up a Mock Chicken Cacciatore ($11.95) on rice or pasta that is large enough for leftovers the next day. The Spinach Citrus Salad ($6.95) is a nondairy treat, with a wine vinaigrette instead of the standard bacon dressing that ruins so many spinach salads. The Sloppy Jose ($6.95) is made with mock taco meat and a mock meat spaghetti sauce. Salads, soups, pizzas, and sandwiches round out the menu, with many not-necessarily-healthy but tasty appetizers. Nondairy dishes are clearly marked, as are those with fish. Slice of Life won't make menu substitutions, but there should still be enough on the menu from which to choose.

VEGETARIAN WITH MANY NONDAIRY OFFERINGS; FISH ALSO SERVED

★★ / $$
20. Sweet Tomatoes

2351 Willow Road
Glenview, IL, 60025
847.657.8141
www.sweettomatoes.com

AMERICAN

Hours:	Sun-Th 11:00 a.m. to 9:00 p.m.
	Fri-Sat 11:00 a.m. to 10:00 p.m.
Payment:	Credit cards accepted
Parking:	Free lot
Alcohol:	No
Atmosphere:	Cafeteria chain

Other locations:
1951 East McConnor Parkway, Schaumburg, IL 60173, 847.619.1271
See also Collar Counties on page 170

Combine a tempting all-you-can-eat menu plus a can't-beat-that price and the result is Sweet Tomatoes. There's a choreography to dining at Sweet Tomatoes. First act: the salad shuffle. Start with an impressive array of items like squash strips, red beets, and pine nuts, or create a base of freshly tossed or prepared salads and go from there. Then hit the hot foods: pastas, soups, chilis, and more. For the finale, dessert: soft-serve ice cream, brownies, cookies, muffins. Many items, especially at the salad bar, are seasonal; visit the Web site to check the day's fare and even its nutritional information. Signs detail ingredients and helpfully indicate which are vegetarian, since dishes like the rosemary garlic soup and even some prepared salads contain meat or meat products. The manager has complete ingredient lists for all dishes; just ask. Lunch, $7.99; dinner, $9.29; drinks extra.

FULL MENU WITH MANY VEGETARIAN OFFERINGS

★ / $$
21. Thyme and Honey Restaurant and Lounge

100–104 South Oak Park Avenue
Oak Park, IL 60302
708.386.2332

MULTIETHNIC

Hours:	Daily 6:00 a.m. to 10:30 p.m.
Payment:	Credit cards accepted
Parking:	City of Oak Park pay lot in the rear, metered street parking
Alcohol:	BYO, no corkage fee
Atmosphere:	Family-friendly casual

Thyme and Honey, if nothing else, is the perfect microcosm of suburban Oak Park. One part hippie, one part family restaurant, one part lounge, one part hip breakfast spot, Thyme and Honey has a little something for everyone. That means vegetarians who don't even like to think about meat should stay away; steaks and chops are featured alongside the vegetarian-friendly salads, sandwiches, omelettes, and pasta. But the Breami, made of braised eggplant and cubanella peppers ($6.99), is a local favorite, as is the Veggie Burger ($5.99) and the Vegetarian Casserole and Eggs with Steamed Broccoli ($6.99). Thyme and Honey is essentially one step up from a diner, but the offerings are solid. While Thyme and Honey is lined with many windows along busy Oak Park Avenue, the interior is still fairly dark.

FULL MENU WITH MANY VEGETARIAN OFFERINGS

★★ / $
22. Udupi Palace

730 Schaumburg Road
Schaumburg, IL 60173
847.884.9510
www.udupipalace.com

SOUTH INDIAN

Hours: Daily 11:30 a.m. to 9:45 p.m.
Payment: Credit cards accepted
Parking: Free lot
Alcohol: BYO, no corkage fee
Atmosphere: Suburban outpost of small chain

Other locations:
See North Side on page 80

Upudi Palace's city location is consistently named as a favorite among the many vegetarian restaurants that dot Devon Avenue. This suburban location—convenient to Schaumburg's many office parks—enjoys a similar reputation. Instead of the typical all-you-can-eat Indian buffets, Udupi offers reasonably priced lunch specials ($5.95 to $7.95), as well as dishes from its ample and moderately priced menu. Save the pappadam ($1.50) for another restaurant. It is bland and uninteresting. Instead, try one of the several special thalis. The pullav rice dishes are a tasty alternative to lentils and dosai, although the dosai is a solid performer here, too.

VEGETARIAN AND SOME VEGAN OPTIONS

★ / $
23. Vitality Natural Foods

1100 Central Avenue
Wilmette, IL 60091
847.853.4200
www.vitalitynaturalfoods.com

MULTIETHNIC

Hours:	Mon-Sat. 10:00 a.m. to 5:00 p.m. Closed Sun
Payment:	Credit cards accepted
Parking:	Metered street parking
Alcohol:	No
Atmosphere:	Upscale juice bar

A small cafe and juice bar nestled in front of a natural products store and yoga studio, Vitality is a health nut's dream. A few seats look out on Wilmette's quaint downtown. Sit there and order a glass from a large selection of organic juices or lactose-free, homemade soy or almond milk. Follow with any selection from an impressive cafe menu. Choose made-to-order salads from a sanitary salad bar ($7 per pound) or opt for the Goodwich ($5), the house special with avocado, cucumber, tomato, and a honey-mustard spread. The Not Tuna sandwich ($5) is flavored with red pepper and celery and served on whole wheat bread. Pastas and appetizers round out the menu.

VEGAN; SOME DISHES MAY INCLUDE HONEY OR WHEY

Collar Counties

★★★ / $
1. Arbor Vitae Java and Juice

    111 West Jackson
    Naperville, IL 60540
    630.778.9090
    630.778.9093 (faxed orders)

MULTIETHNIC

Hours:	Mon-Th 6:00 a.m. to 9:00 p.m.
	Fri 6:00 a.m. to 10:00 p.m.
	Sat 7:00 a.m. to 11:00 p.m.
	Sun 7:00 a.m. to 9:00 p.m.
	Summer hours: one hour later
Payment:	Credit cards accepted
Parking:	Street parking
Alcohol:	No
Atmosphere:	Coffee shop and juice bar

Step in the door of this warm, eclectic coffee shop and you'll feel right at home. Golden walls are accented with colorful artwork produced by local artists, and fourteen tables offer plenty of seating. Pans of wheatgrass used for smoothies and the enormous coffee bean roaster (all coffee is roasted on the premises) add authentic flair; shelves of books and board games offer a diversion while you sip your berry extreme smoothie, a medley of blackberries, blueberries, raspberries, and strawberries ($3.99). Unlike many coffee shops, Arbor Vitae offers full meals made with all natural and organic ingredients when possible. Try the spinach pie ($2.50), baba ghanooj ($7.20 per pound), or low-fat vegetarian burrito ($4.95), all three of which are flavorful and above average. Veggie chili with an organic green salad ($4.80) is a good bet for a cold day, with just the right amount of heat. Owners Fran and Bill Pryor's friendly demeanor keeps locals coming in all year long.

CAFE MENU WITH MANY VEGETARIAN OFFERINGS

★★★ / $$
2. bd's mongolian barbeque

445 East Townline Road
Vernon Hills, IL 60061
847.247.9600

PAN-ASIAN

Hours:	Mon-Th 11:00 a.m. to 10:00 p.m.
	Fri-Sat 11:00 a.m. to 11:00 p.m.
	Sun noon to 9:00 p.m.
Payment:	Credit cards accepted
Parking:	Free lot
Alcohol:	Full bar with many specialty drinks
Atmosphere:	Midscale, DIY chain

Other locations:
221 Washington, Naperville, IL 60540,
630.428.0300
See also North Side on page 28

With its kitsch and its T.G.I. Friday's–style drinks and dessert menu, it'd be easy to write this place off as yet another chain and go somewhere independent or more authentic. That would be a mistake. For $11.99 at lunch and $13.99 at dinner, you can help yourself to an all-you-can-eat series of trips to the barbeque, where you pile on your own stir-fry and sauces, and a chef cooks it on the grill, separating vegetarian bowls from those of meat-eaters. (Vegans and those with allergies can request their meals be fried in a separate pan.) The ingredients line includes many savory sauces, including an excellent black bean, with directions on the best ways to combine ingredients. When it comes to the meat area, a sign reads, "Vegetarians may advance to Step 2." Lower prices are available for one-trip servings and kid portions, and since everyone makes his or her own dish from fresh ingredients, there is no cause for complaints.

VEGETARIAN AND VEGAN OFFERINGS; MEAT, FISH, POULTRY, AND SEAFOOD ALSO SERVED

★★ / $
3. Fitness Cafe

164 Danada West
Wheaton, IL 60187
630.588.8551

MULTIETHNIC

Hours:	Mon-Sat 11:00 a.m. to 8:00 p.m. (summer, to 9:00 p.m.) Closed Sun
Payment:	Credit cards accepted
Parking:	Free lot in front
Alcohol:	No
Atmosphere:	Fitness-theme cafe

Other locations:
See Suburban Cook County on page 142

The climbing wall and dumbbell-shaped counter make Fitness Cafe seem a bit like eating at the gym, minus the treadmills and sweaty guys in tank tops. But don't let the utilitarian atmosphere throw you—the food's delicious, and if you're watching your diet, you'll find plenty of options. The menu, posted on the wall, gives complete calorie counts for each item, as well as carbs, fat, and protein grams. Except for the low-carb menu, every food category—cold and hot sandwiches, wraps, pastas, kids' specials, and salads—has at least one vegetarian option. Sandwiches include the Free Style, layering grilled portobello mushrooms, cucumbers, avocados, tomatoes, red onions, and fresh organic greens, served with your choice of cheese on cracked whole wheat bread with special ranch dressing ($5.99 for a mere 355 calories). Or try the penne pasta with red and green peppers, diced portobello mushrooms, onions, and tomatoes ($5.99).

FULL MENU WITH VEGETARIAN OFFERINGS

★ / $
4. Frullati Cafe

Fox Valley Shopping Center
184 Westfield
Aurora, IL 60504
630.585.8991
www.frullati.com

SNACKS AND SMOOTHIES

Hours:	Mon-Sat 10:00 a.m. to 9:00 p.m.
	Sun 11:00 a.m. to 6:00 p.m.
Payment:	ATM or debit cards accepted
Parking:	Free mall lot
Alcohol:	No
Atmosphere:	Fast food

In the basement-level food court at the former Fox Valley Mall (now Westfield), Frullati Cafe serves up a 20-ounce cup of frothy carrot juice, along with many other drinks for the fruit-minded. Or get a straight glass of fresh juice such as apple, orange, guava, watermelon, lemonade, and raspberry or strawberry lemonade. The smoothies are nondairy and use juice, not fruit chunks. From the many flavor combos, try the delicious guava-mango. The menu's sweet smoothies include mocha java, Oreo, Butterfinger, and Hershey's chocolate, while the fruit chillers are strawberry-based slushies with crushed ice, fruit, and juice. Add extra boosters like protein powder, ginseng, wheatgrass, spirulina, multivitamins, or bee pollen for 60 cents each. For a decent meal with your beverage, the Veggie Veneto sandwich is a good bet, stacking lettuce, tomato, black olives, avocado, cucumbers, onions, and provolone cheese. Juices $1.59 to $5.25; sandwiches $3 to $5.

FULL MENU WITH MANY VEGETARIAN AND VEGAN DRINK OPTIONS

★★ / $$
5. Jalapeño's

7 Clock Tower Plaza
Elgin, IL 60120
847.468.9445

MEXICAN

Hours: Daily 9:00 a.m. to 10:00 p.m.
Payment: Credit cards accepted
Parking: Free lot
Alcohol: Full bar
Atmosphere: Family-friendly suburban restaurant and nightclub

After you've lost a few bucks at Elgin's Grand Victoria Casino, a safe bet for a decent veggie pick-me-up is just across the way at Jalapeño's in the Clock Tower Plaza. The kitchen does a fantastic job with the eight-slice portobello quesadilla appetizer ($7.25), which is large enough for a light meal. The vegetarian combo platter ($10.25), consisting of a cheese burrito, guacamole tostada, and a cheese-and-onion enchilada, is also satisfyingly filling. As if that weren't enough food, it comes with sides of refried beans and rice. For an extra 75 cents, switch out one or two of the platter's main components for either a quesadilla or cheese chili relleno (poblano pepper, stuffed, breaded, and fried). For dessert, try mulitas ($3.25), Mexico's deep-fried answer to crepes. The breakfast and lunch buffet menus change daily but always have basic vegetarian fare (think pancakes and salad), and the kitchen is amenable to off-menu requests. An adjoining nightclub features karaoke on some nights and live music most Friday and Saturday nights.

FULL MENU WITH MANY VEGETARIAN OPTIONS

★★ / $$
6. Mysore Woodlands

6020 South Cass Avenue
Westmont, IL 60559
630.769.9663

SOUTH INDIAN

Hours: Daily 11:30 a.m. to 9:00 p.m.
Payment: Credit cards accepted
Parking: Free parking lot
Alcohol: BYO, no corkage fee
Atmosphere: Midscale

Other locations:
See North Side on page 63

If you're used to the usual array of dishes found at most Indian restaurants, you will find some wonderful surprises at Mysore Woodlands, which specializes in the harder-to-find cuisine of southern India. While its all-vegetarian menu contains a few familiar items that you might find anywhere, the better choices (and bigger bargains) are found among the house specialties. Start with one of several varieties of veda (fried lentil doughnuts), alu banda (lentil dumpling with potato and onion), or a bowl of sour and spicy rasam soup ($2.50 to $4.50). For lunch or a simpler dinner, have one of several varieties of uttapam, pancakes topped with your choice of onions, chiles, peas, or other vegetables ($6 to $7). Or instead, have a dosai (rice crepe) stuffed with tasty fillings like chutney, potatoes, or lentils ($6 to $12). More ambitious entrées are also available such as the popular pongal avail featuring mashed rice and lentils in a spicy sauce. If you're very hungry (or in a mood to experiment and share), order a combination thali.

VEGETARIAN

★★ / $
7. Noodles and Company

137 North Weber Road
Bolingbrook, IL 60440
630.771.9999
www.noodles.com

MULTIETHNIC

Hours:	Sun-Wed 11:00 a.m. to 9:00 p.m.
	Th-Sat 11:00 a.m. to 10:00 p.m.
Payment:	Credit cards accepted
Parking:	Free lot
Alcohol:	Beer and Wine
Atmosphere:	Midscale chain

Other locations:
4912 Northwest Hwy, Crystal Lake, IL 60014, 815.459.4400
895 South Randall Road, Elgin, IL 60123, 847.888.0500
1310 Commons Drive, Geneva, IL 60134, 630.262.6400
207 South Washington Avenue, Naperville, IL 60540, 630.369.3332
2019 South Naperville Road, Wheaton, IL 60187, 630.221.0011
See also Suburban Cook County on page 152

Italian, Japanese, Thai, and other cuisines are represented here, all by dishes with noodles as a primary ingredient. The Wisconsin mac 'n' cheese ($3.70 or $4.95) has fans who choose it over homemade. The Japanese pan noodles ($5.50) and the Indonesian peanut sauté ($5.75) both have strong flavors and are served in ample portions. If you aren't happy with your choice, a staff member happily brings you another entrée at no charge. While you order at the counter, your dishes are served to you at your table.

MOSTLY VEGETARIAN; CHICKEN, MEAT, AND FISH ALSO SERVED

★★ / $
8. Roly Poly Sandwiches

1306 Commons Drive
Geneva, IL 60134
630.232.8190
www.rolypolyusa.com

American

Hours:	Mon-Sat 10:00 a.m. to 9:00 p.m.
	Sun 11:00 a.m. to 6:00 p.m.
Payment:	Credit cards accepted
Parking:	Free lot
Alcohol:	No
Atmosphere:	Casual mall fast-food restaurant

This tidy wrap shop is an economical island in a sea of pricier restaurants in the upscale Geneva Commons outdoor mall. The "original hand-rolled sandwiches" at Roly Poly's taste refreshingly fresh—a great place for shoppers to rest and refuel. Ingredients are rolled up in your choice of a wheat or white wrap; about a third of the vegetarian selections are grilled. These "toasted" choices, as the menu calls them, include the tasty Veggie Fajita (melted cheddar and jalapeno jack cheese plus spinach, tomatoes, green peppers, and other veggies). Untoasted, the delicious Nut and Honey Wrap combines cream cheese, avocado, spinach, carrots, nuts, raisins, lettuce, tomato, and honey mustard dressing. Calorie-counters should try the Ultimate Veggie Wrap, a low-fat option that includes artichoke hearts, roasted red peppers, and green peppers with fat-free ranch dressing. To design your wrap, choose one of six cheeses and then six selections from a list of sixteen vegetables, dressings (skip the Caesar), and spreads such as hummus, cranberry sauce, or mango chutney. Whole wraps run $4.75 to $5.35; the sizeable half-wraps cost $3.25.

FULL MENU WITH VEGETARIAN OFFERINGS

★★★ / $$
9. Sri Ganesh

837 East Roosevelt Road
Lombard, IL 60148
630.620.9175
www.sriganeshcuisine.com

INDIAN

Hours:	Tue-Fri 11:30 a.m. to 2:30 p.m., 5:30 p.m. to 9:30 p.m.
	Sat 11:30 a.m. to 3:00 p.m., 5:30 p.m. to 11:30 p.m.
	Sun 11:30 a.m. to 3:00 p.m., 5:30 p.m. to 10:00 p.m.
	Closed Mon
Payment:	Credit cards accepted
Parking:	Free lot
Alcohol:	BYO, no corkage fee
Atmosphere:	Family-friendly midscale

One of the few completely meat-free suburban restaurants, Sri Ganesh employs a talented chef with more than three decades' experience in Indian cuisine. Start with the aloo tiki appetizer ($4.45), which is two spicy and perfectly shaped potato-lentil patties accompanied by several dipping sauces. The samosa appetizer ($1.95) is a fantastic bargain, serving up two of the most enormous samosas you're likely to ever see. The Mysore Masala Dosai's spicy onion-and-potato chutney filling is eye-wateringly spicy. One of the smooth lassi yogurt drinks ($1.75) is a cool balance, as is the saffron pista ice cream ($2.45), three small scoops of a green, pistachio-flavored treat with a powerful, flowery aroma. The lunch buffet ($6.95), with its rotating selection of curries, rice dishes, and other goodies like puffed bread poori (think of a tortilla balloon), is a great way to sample. The gracious staff accommodates special requests, happily makes recommendations, and offers menu explanations.

VEGETARIAN WITH SOME VEGAN OPTIONS

★★★ / $$
10. Swagat Indian Cuisine

1570 West Ogden Avenue
Naperville, IL 60540
630.420.7565

INDIAN

Hours:	Mon-Th 11:30 a.m. to 2:30 p.m., 5:00 p.m. to 9:30 p.m.
	Fri 11:00 a.m. to 2:30 p.m. 5:00 p.m. to 10:00 p.m.
	Sat noon to 3:00 p.m., 5:00 p.m. to 10:00 p.m.
	Sun noon to 3:00 p.m., 5:00 p.m. to 9:30 p.m.
Payment:	Credit cards accepted
Parking:	Free lot
Alcohol:	BYO, no corkage fee
Atmosphere:	Midscale family restaurant

A great find for suburban vegetarians, this friendly, family-owned restaurant opened its doors New Year's Day 2004. Hidden at the end of the Jefferson Square Complex strip mall in Naperville's car dealership district, Swagat should not be judged by its location or its unattractive exterior. For a fantastic deal, go for one of the weekday lunch specials. Try the idly/vada/dosa combo for $4.95 (the same specials are $1 more on weekend lunches and $3 more on the dinner menu). Vegetarian dinner options are extensive: 19 appetizers, 19 curries, 19 kinds of dosai or uttapam, and several soups, paneers, and other specialties. The popular Mysore Masala Dosai ($6.95) is appropriately spicy. The friendly staff reflects the restaurant's name, which translates as "welcome" in Sanskrit. Feel free to ask for recommendations and explanations, or to request something not on the menu.

MOSTLY VEGETARIAN WITH SOME VEGAN OPTIONS

★★ / $$
11. Sweet Tomatoes

2801 East Main Street
St. Charles, IL 60174
630.377.3309
www.sweettomatoes.com

AMERICAN

Hours:	Sun-Th 11:00 a.m. to 9:00 p.m.
	Fri-Sat 11:00 a.m. to 10:00 p.m.
Payment:	Credit cards accepted
Parking:	Free lot
Alcohol:	No
Atmosphere:	Cafeteria chain

Other locations:
See Suburban Cook County on page 155

Combine a tempting all-you-can-eat menu plus a can't-beat-that price and the result is Sweet Tomatoes. There's a choreography to dining at Sweet Tomatoes, a kind of buffet ballet. First act: the salad shuffle. Start from scratch with an impressive array of items like squash strips, red beets, and pine nuts, or create a base of freshly tossed or prepared salads and go from there. Then hit the hot foods: pastas, soups, chilis, and more. For the finale, dessert: soft-serve ice cream, brownies, cookies, muffins. Many items, especially at the salad bar, are seasonal; visit the Web site to check the day's fare and even its nutritional information. Signs above the sneeze-guards detail ingredients and helpfully indicate which are vegetarian, since dishes like the rosemary garlic soup and even some prepared salads contain meat or meat products. The manager has complete ingredient lists for all dishes; just ask. Lunch, $7.99; dinner, $9.29; drinks extra.

**FULL MENU WITH MANY
VEGETARIAN OFFERINGS**

★★ / $$
12. Thai Spice

1234 North Lake Street
Aurora, IL 60506
630.264.9904

THAI

Hours:	Tue-Th 11:00 a.m. to 3:00 p.m., 4:30 p.m. to 9:00 p.m.
	Fri-Sat 11:00 a.m. to 10:00 p.m.
	Sun 3:30 p.m. to 9:00 p.m.
	Closed Mon
Payment:	Credit cards accepted
Parking:	Free lot
Alcohol:	Beer and wine only
Atmosphere:	Midscale

Thai Spice is a first-rate suburban strip-mall spot, and under new management the restaurant has flourished. The deep-fried egg roll appetizers ($3.95) are a great way to start (happily, the kitchen uses vegetable oil). The three rolls are on the small side, so you won't fill up before your main course, and the hard, crunchy shells are a slightly different take on traditional softer wraps. If you're in the mood for something light, try a steaming bowl of the outstanding tom kha soup ($6.95), a savory broth with loads of flavor. The pad thai ($7.25) is par for the course, but the yellow curry ($7.95) shines with a gentle kick and generous helpings of red peppers, potatoes, and onions. Peanut lovers should definitely try the panang curry ($7.95). True to the restaurant's name, many dishes can be as spicy as you dare; just tell your server your spice-level preference. Most nonveggie dishes can be ordered with tofu or vegetables. Enormous portions mean that most diners leave with doggy bags in hand.

FULL MENU WITH MANY VEGETARIAN AND VEGAN OFFERINGS

★ / $$
13. Yummy Bowl

1908 Sheridan Road
Highland Park, IL 60035
847.266.8880

CHINESE/THAI

Hours:	Mon-Th 11:30 a.m. to 9:00 p.m.
	Fri-Sat 11:30 a.m. to 10:00 p.m.
	Sun 4:00 p.m. to 9:00 p.m.
Payment:	Credit cards accepted
Parking:	Street parking
Alcohol:	Full bar
Atmosphere:	Family-friendly midscale

Despite the inelegant name and nothing-fancy atmosphere, Yummy Bowl has some of the best Asian food in the North Shore area, and is a favorite with families. Walls are painted happy colors of sunny yellow, rich red, and mango, and on busy nights, a player piano entertains. The all-English menu makes ordering easy and even includes Caesar salad and spaghetti. But the good stuff is the Chinese and Thai, both done with flair. Traditional favorites include cashew chicken that's made vegetarian with tofu or vegetables. A must-try is the eggplant in rich plum sauce, stirred with baby corn, peppers, and onions. Kung bao with tofu is a sweet combo of red and green peppers, peanuts, onions, and sliced zucchini. Garlic tofu noodles, served in a boat-shaped bowl, are pleasantly spicy with cilantro and brown sauce. Whatever you order, you'll likely fight over leftovers. Vegetarian lunch specials are a bargain at $4.95. Entrées $7.95 to $12.95.

FULL MENU WITH MANY VEGETARIAN AND VEGAN OFFERINGS

Resources

Chicago Vegetarian Society
P.O. Box 223
Highwood, IL 60040
847.561.1302
www.chicagovegetariansoc.org

ChicaGourmets!
708.383.7543
www.chicagourmets.com
Local food and wine society.

The Chopping Block
www.thechoppingblock.net
Cooking school with two locations and hands-on vegetarian cooking sources:

   4747 N. Lincoln Ave.
   Chicago, IL 60625
   773.472.6700

   1324 W. Webster Ave.
   Chicago, IL 60614
   773.472.6700

Conscious Choice
920 N. Franklin St., Suite 202
Chicago, IL 60610
312.440.4373
www.consciouschoice.com
Monthly magazine covering local sustainability issues.

EarthSave Chicago
chicago.earthsave.org
Promotes vegetarian lifestyles through potlucks and hosting regular speakers.

Enchanted Kitchens
1207 Hohlfelder Rd.
Glencoe, IL 60002
773.347.1215
www.enchantedkitchens.com
Raw food preparation and vegetarian cooking classes.

Go Veggie!
P.O. Box 577997
Chicago, IL 60657
773.871.7000
www.go-veggie.org
Provides coupons on regular events for local members.

Healthy Dining Club
312.666.9979
HealthyDining@aol.com
Dining club for health-conscious adults.

In a Vegetarian Kitchen
www.VegKitchen.com

Local Organic Initiative
920 N. Franklin St., Suite 301
Chicago, IL 60610
312.951.8999
www.sustainusa.org/
   localorganic
Supports the growth of a regional food system in Illinois, Wisconsin, Michigan, and Indiana; a project of Sustain.

Organic Food Network
P.O. Box 4086
Wheaton, IL 60189
630.836.1864
OFN2@aol.com

The Raw Vegan Network
www.therawvegannetwork.com

Vegan Action
www.vegan.org

Vegan Outreach/
  Protecting Animals USA
P.O. Box 25097
Chicago, IL 60625
www.veganoutreach.org

VegChicago
www.vegchicago.com

VegDining.com
www.vegdining.com

Veg Source
www.vegsource.com

Vegetarian and Organic
  Friendly, Too! (VO2)
VO2Chicago@aol.com
Bimonthly newsletter with
Chicago-area events.

Yoga Chicago
P.O. Box 607447
Chicago, IL 60660
www.yogachicago.com
Monthly magazine.

Community-Supported Agriculture (CSA)

CSAs allow individuals to buy a share of a local farm, typically one that grows organic produce, in exchange for a delivery of what is harvested that week.

Angelic Organics
1547 Rockton Rd.
Caledonia, IL 61011
815.389.2746
www.angelicorganics.com

Cedar Valley Sustainable
1985 N. 3609th Rd.
Ottawa, IL 61350
815.431.9544

Green Earth Institute
10S404 Knoch Knolls Rd.
Naperville, IL 60565
630.717.1950
www.greenearthinstitute.org

Home Grown Wisconsin
211 Canal Rd.
Waterloo, WI 53594
608.341.8939
www.homegrownwisconsin.com

King's Hill Farm
19370 County Road G
Mineral Point, WI 53565
888.752.2301
www.kingshillfarm.com

Prospera Farm
W3566 County Road E
Berlin, WI 54923
920.361.4747
www.prosperafarm.com

Rainbow Farmers Cooperative
5500 W. Silver Spring Rd.
Milwaukee, WI 53218
414.527.1546
www.growingpower.org

Sandhill Organics at Prairie Crossing
32140 N. Harris Rd.
Grayslake, IL 60030
847.548.4030
www.sandhillorganics.com

Scotch Hill Farm
910 Scotch Hill Rd.
Broadhead, WI 53520
608.897.4288
scotchhillfarm@wekz.net

Sweet Earth Organic Farm
53652 County Road N.
Wauzeka, WI 53826
608.875.6026
www.sweetearthorganicfarm.com

Worm Farm
E7904 Briar Bluff Rd.
Reedsburg, WI 53959
608.524.8678
wormfarm@jvlnet.com

Juice Bars

North Side
Crunch Chicago
939 W. North Ave.
Chicago IL 60622
312.337.1244
www.crunch.com

Energia Juice Bar
Cheetah Gym
www.cheetahgym.com

  5248 N. Clark St.
  Chicago, IL 60640
  773.728.7777

  1934 W. North Ave.
  Chicago, IL 60622
  773.394.5900

Fresh Choice
3351 N. Broadway Ave.
Chicago, IL 60657
773.248.5000

Frullati Café
1030 N. Clark St.
Chicago, IL 60610
312.337.8700
www.frullati.com

Jamba Juice
www.jambajuice.com

  2800 N. Clark St.
  Chicago, IL 60657
  773.755.8472

  2112B N. Clybourn Ave.
  Chicago, IL 60614
  773.244.1260

  1571 N. Sheffield Ave.
  Chicago, IL 60622
  312.280.1945

  30 W. Huron St.,
    (in Whole Foods)
  Chicago, IL 60610
  312.932.9600

Jubilee Juice
140 N. Halsted St.
Chicago, IL 60661
312.491.8500

Karyn's Cafe
1901 N. Halsted St.
Chicago, IL 60614
312.255.1590

Life Spring Health Foods
  and Juice Bar
3178 N. Clark St.
Chicago, IL 60657
773.327.1023

Planet Smoothie
852 W. Belmont Ave.
Chicago, IL 60657
773.929.3850
www.planetsmoothie.com

Quad's Gym and Juice Bar
3727 N. Broadway Ave.
Chicago, IL 60613
773.404.7867

Downtown
Brian's Juice Bar and Deli
80 E. Lake St.
Chicago, IL 60601
312.332.3435

Crunch Chicago
350 N. State St.
Chicago, IL 60610
312.527.8100
www.crunch.com

Fresh Choice
1534 N. Wells St.
Chicago, IL 60610
312.664.7065

Frullati Café
Merchandise Mart
222 Merchandise Mart Plaza
Suite 205
Chicago, IL 60654
312.245.9282
www.frullati.com

Jamba Juice
www.jambajuice.com

   Merchandise Mart
   222 Merchandise Mart Plaza
   Chicago, IL 60654
   312.321.0470

   20 N. Michigan Ave.
     Suite 101
   Chicago, IL 60602
   312.726.7281

   John Hancock Center
   875 N. Michigan Ave.
   Chicago, IL 60611
   312.440.9824

   166 N. State St.
   Chicago, IL 60601
   312.641.1925

   225 S. Canal (in Union
     Station)
   Chicago, IL 60606
   312.382.9904

   209 W. Jackson St.
   Chicago, IL 60606
   312.235.0306

   190 W. Madison St.
   Chicago, IL 60602
   312.357.1041

   500 W. Madison St.
     (in Citicorp Center #C007)
   Chicago, IL 60661
   312.474.0350

Kramers Health Foods
230 S. Wabash Ave.
Chicago, IL 60604
312.922.0077

Maple St. Market
22 W. Maple St.
Chicago, IL 60610
312.397.1501

Miracle Juice Bar/Foodlife
Water Tower Place, Mezzanine
835 N. Michigan Ave.
Chicago, IL 60611
312.335.3663
www.leye.com

South Side

Bonne Sante Health Food
1512 E. 53rd St.
Chicago, IL 60615
773.667.5700

Eternity Juice Bar and Deli
203 E. 75th St.
Chicago, IL 60619
773.224.0104

Hyde Park Coop
   1226 E. 53rd St.
   Chicago, IL 60615
   773.363.2175

   1526 E. 55th St.
   Chicago, IL 60615
   773.667.1444

I.C.Y. Vegetarian Restaurant
   and Juice Bar
3141 W. Roosevelt Road
Chicago, IL 60612
773.762.1090

Jamba Juice
1322 S. Halsted St.
Chicago, IL 60607
312.738.3660
www.jambajuice.com

S.town Health Foods
2100 W. 95th St.
Chicago, IL 60643
773.233.1856

Suburban Cook County
Chowpatti International
 Vegetarian Cuisine
1035 S. Arlington Heights Rd.
Arlington Heights, IL 60005
847.640.9554

Frullati Café
www.frullati.com

Prairie Stone Sports &
 Wellness Center

5050 Sedge Blvd.
Hoffman Estates, IL 60192
847.285.5400

4142 N. Harlem Ave.
Norridge, IL 60706
708.456.4833

2326 Northbrook Court
Northbrook, IL 60062
847.272.7183

Orland Square Mall
288 Orland Square Dr.,
 Space C-11
Orland Park, IL 60462
708.403.1099

1760 N. Hicks Rd.
Palatine, IL 60074
847.991.4646

5 Woodfield Mall,
 Space D-205
Schaumburg, IL 60173

Jamba Juice
www.jambajuice.com

630 Davis St., #101
Evanston, IL 60201
847.425.1740

Sts. of Woodfield
601 N. Martingale Rd.,
 #310
Schaumburg, IL 60173
847.995.1445

Planet Smoothie
49 Summit Ave.
Park Ridge, IL 60068
847.825.0255

3232 Lake Ave.
Wilmette, IL 60091
847.251.2975

Vitality Natural Foods
1100 Central Ave.
Wilmette, IL 60091
847.853.4200

**Collar Counties:
DuPage, Kane, Lake,
McHenry, Will**
Arbor Vitae Java and Juice
111 W. Jackson Ave.
Naperville, IL
630.778.9090

Fitness Cafe
164 Danada W.
Wheaton, IL, 60187
630.588.8551

Frullati Cafe
www.frullati.com

   184 Westfield (Fox Valley)
     Shopping Center, BTQ-1
   Aurora, IL 60504
   630.585.8991

   Good Shepherd Hospital
     Health and Fitness Center
   1301 S. Barrington Rd.
   Barrington, IL 60010
   847.620.4542

   Stratford Mall
   152 Stratford Square
   Bloomingdale, IL 60108
   630.307.0179

   Buffalo Grove Fitness Center
   601 Deerfield Parkway
   Buffalo Grove, IL 60089
   847.353.7554

   96 River Oaks Center
     Space D37-37
   Calumet City, IL 60409
   708.868.2651

   Gurnee Mills
   6170 Grand Ave., Space 231
   Gurnee, IL 60031
   847.855.9080

   Health & Fitness Institute
   3098 Falling Waters Blvd.
   Lindenhurst, IL 60046
   847.535.7644

   Gas City
   12502 W. 143rd St.
   Lockport, IL 60441
   708.645.0370

Gas City
   900 Brook Forest Ave.
   Shorewood, IL 60431
   815.744.9990

   903 Hawthorne Shopping
     Center, Space FF3-UL
   Vernon Hills, IL 60061
   847.680.7886

   1077 Springhill Mall
   West Dundee, IL 60118
   847.428.8756

   Willowbrook Athletic Club
   215 W. 63rd St.
   Willowbrook, IL 60527
   630.323.3918

Jamba Juice
www.jambajuice.com

   Geneva Commons
   1544 Commons Dr.
   Geneva, IL 60134
   630.262.9455

   1849 Green Bay Rd.
   Highland Park, IL 60035
   847.266.8121

   Lincolnshire City Park
   275 Parkway Dr.
   Lincolnshire, IL 60069
   847.353.8004

   17 W. 22nd St.
   Villa Park, IL 60181
   630.279.5332

   Cantera Commons
   28341 Diehl Rd.
   Warrenville, IL 60555
   630.393.0159

   Murphy's Health Foods
     and Juice Bar
   400 N. Milwaukee Ave.
   Libertyville, IL 60048
   847.362.4664

FARMERS MARKETS

Get more information about Chicago's Downtown, S., W., and N. Side farmers markets on the city's Events page at www.cityofchicago.org or by calling 312.744.3315.

Downtown

Cooking and Hospitality
Institute of Chicago (CHIC)
Market
361 W. Chestnut St.
773.779.5055
Weekly,
Sun 9:00 a.m. to 1:00 p.m.
Year-round; call for dates of
   periodic closures
Parking lot in warm weather,
   inside the school in winter

Daley Plaza
Washington and Dearborn Sts.
Weekly,
Th 7:00 a.m. to 3:00 p.m.
Mid-May to late September

Federal Plaza
Adams and Dearborn Sts.
Weekly,
Tue 7:00 a.m. to 3:00 p.m.
Mid-May to mid-October

Maxwell St. Market
Canal St. and Roosevelt Rd.
Weekly,
Sun 7:00 a.m. to 3:00 p.m.
Year-round

Museum of Contemporary
Art/St.erville
Chicago Ave. and
   Mies van der Rohe Way,
   (on the museum plaza)
Weekly,
Tue 10:00 a.m. to 6:00 p.m.
Mid-June to mid-October

The Park at Jackson and Wacker
311 S. Wacker Dr.
Weekly,
Th 7:00 a.m. to 3:00 p.m.
Mid-June to late October

Printers Row
Polk and Dearborn Sts.
Weekly,
Sat 7:00 a.m. to 2:00 p.m.
Mid-June to late October

Prudential Plaza
Prudential Building Plaza
Lake St. and Beaubien Ct.
Weekly,
Tue 7:00 a.m. to 3:00 p.m.
Mid-June to mid-October

W. Loop
843 W. Randolph St.
Courtyard next to Marche
Restaurant
Weekly, Th 4:00 to 8:00 p.m.
Late June to late October

South Side

Ashburn
87th St. and Kedzie Ave.
Brown's Chicken parking lot
Weekly,
Sat 8:00 a.m. to 1:00 p.m.
Mid-June to late October

Beverly
95th St. and Longwood Dr.
City parking lot, SE corner
Weekly,
Sun 7:00 a.m. to 2:00 p.m.
Late May to late October

Bronzeville
30th St. and
  Martin Luther King Dr.
Dunbar Vocational Career
  Academy parking lot
Weekly,
Sat 7:00 a.m. to 2:00 p.m.
Mid-June to late October

Gately/Pullman
111th St. and
  S. Cottage Grove Ave.
Arcade Park
Weekly,
Wed 7:00 a.m. to 2:00 p.m.
Mid-June to mid-October

Hyde Park
52nd Place and Harper Ave.
  (on the cul-de-sac at
  Harper Court)
Weekly,
Th 7:00 a.m. to 2:00 p.m.
Mid-June to mid-October

Lawndale
Grenshaw St. and Homan Ave.
Community Bank of Lawndale
  parking lot
Weekly,
Wed 7:00 a.m. to 2:00 p.m.
Mid-June to mid-October

Morgan Park
92nd St. and Ashland Ave.
Shiloah M. B. Church
  parking lot
Weekly,
Sat 7:00 a.m. to 2:00 p.m.
Mid-June to late October

South Shore
70th St. and S. Jeffery Ave.
South Shore Bank parking lot
Weekly,
Wed, 7:00 a.m. to 2:00 p.m.
Mid-June to late October

West Lawn
65th St. and Pulaski Rd.
Republic Bank parking lot
Weekly,
Sun 8:00 a.m. to 1:00 p.m.
Mid-June to late October

West Side

Austin
Madison St. and Central Ave.
Emmet Math, Science
  and Technology Academy
  parking lot
Weekly,
Sat 7:00 a.m. to 2:00 p.m.
Early July to late October

North Side

Chicago's Green City Market
1750 N. Clark St.
  (at Stockton Drive)
www.chicagogreencitymarket.org
Weekly,
Wed 7:00 a.m. to 1:30 p.m.
Mid-May to late October

Dunning, Eli's/Wright College
Montrose and
  Forest Preserve Aves.
Eli's Cheesecake Co. parking lot
Weekly,
Th 7:00 a.m. to 2:00 p.m.
Mid-June to mid-October

Edgewater
Thorndale Ave. and Broadway St.
Broadway Armory parking lot
Weekly,
Sat 7:00 a.m. to 2:00 p.m.
Mid-June to mid-October

Edison/Norwood Park
  Oshkosh Ave. and Northwest
  Hwy. (in parking lot next
  to Edison Park Field House)
Monthly,
Wed 10:00 a.m. to 6:00 p.m.
June to October

Galewood/Montclare
Cortland St. and Newland Ave.
Sayre Language Academy
  parking lot
Monthly,
Sun 8:00 a.m. to 1:00 p.m.
July to October

Garfield Park
Washington Blvd. and Central
  Park Ave. (Garfield Park,
  north of the Conservatory)
Weekly,
Sun 9:00 a.m. to 4:00 p.m.
Mid-June to late October

Lincoln Park
Armitage Ave. and Orchard St.
Lincoln Park High School
  parking lot
Weekly,
Sat 7:00 a.m. to 2:00 p.m.
Mid-May to late October

Lincoln Park Zoo
2001 N. Stockton Dr.,
  (at the Farm in the Zoo)
Monthly,
Sun 9:00 a.m. to 4:00 p.m.
June to September

Lincoln Square
At Lincoln, Leland, and
  Western Aves. (City parking
  lot adjacent to Western
  Brown Line station)
Weekly, Mid-June to late Oct.
Tue 7:00 a.m. to 2:00 p.m.

Near North
Division and Dearborn Sts.
(on Division between State
  and Clark Sts.)
Weekly,
Sat 7:00 a.m. to 2:00 p.m.
Mid-June to mid-October

North Center
North Center Town Square
At Belle Plaine, Damen, and
  Lincoln Aves.
Weekly,
Sat 7:00 a.m. to 2:00 p.m.
Mid-June to mid-October

North Halsted,
Grace, Broadway, and
  Halsted Sts.
Faith Tabernacle Church
  parking lot
Weekly,
Sat 7:00 a.m. to 2:00 p.m.
Mid-June to late October

Rogers Park Community Craft
  and Farmers Market
Howard St. and Ashland Ave.
  (between Rogers Ave. and
  Howard St.)
Weekly,
Sun 10:00 a.m. to 2:00 p.m.
Mid-June to mid-October

Roscoe Village
Belmont and Wolcott Aves.
Friedrich Ludwig Jahn Play Lot
Weekly,
Sun 7:00 a.m. to 2:00 p.m.
Mid-June to late October

Wicker Park/Bucktown
Milwaukee and Damen Aves.
Weekly,
Sun 7:00 a.m. to 2:00 p.m.
Mid-June to late October

Suburban Cook County
Deerfield Farmers Market
Deerfield and Robert York Rds.
  (commuter parking lot at
  the NW corner)
Deerfield, IL
847.945.5000
Weekly,
Sat 7:00 a.m. to 12:30 p.m.
Mid-June to mid-October

Evanston Farmers Market
University Pl. and Oak Ave.
Evanston, IL
847.866.2936
Weekly,
Sat 7:30 a.m. to 1:00 p.m.
Early June to late October

La Grange Farmers Market
53 S. La Grange Rd.
Village of La Grange
   parking lot
La Grange, IL
708.352.0494
Weekly,
Th 7:00 a.m. to 1:00 p.m.
Early June to late October

La Grange Park Farmers
   Market
1215 E. 31st St.
National City Bank parking lot
La Grange Park, IL
708.352.0494
Weekly,
Tue 8:00 a.m. to 2:00 p.m.
Early June to late October

Park Ridge Farmers Market
Garden and Prairie Aves.
   (south of Metro train station)
Park Ridge, IL
847.825.3121
Weekly,
Sat 7:00 a.m. to 1:00 p.m.
Early June to late October

Skokie Farmers Market
5127 Oakton St. (near
   Village Hall)
Skokie, IL
847.673.0500
Weekly,
Sun 7:30 a.m. to 12:45 p.m.
Late June to late October

Wilmette Farmers Market
Central Ave. and Green Bay Rd.
Downtown Wilmette Metra
   parking lot, East
Wilmette, IL
847.251.3800
Weekly,
Sat 9:00 a.m. to 2:00 p.m.
Early June to late October

**Collar Counties:
DuPage, Kane, Lake,
McHenry, Will**

Aurora Farmers Market
233 N. Broadway
Aurora Transportation Center
Aurora, IL
630.844.3640
Weekly, Sat 7:00 a.m. to noon
Early June to late October

Downers Grove Farmers
   Market
Main St. Metro Station, Lot B
Downers Grove, IL
630.968.8400
Weekly, Sat 7:00 a.m. to noon
Mid-June to late October

Grayslake Farmers Market
Center and Slusser Sts.
Grayslake, IL
847.204.0034
Weekly,
Wed 3:00 to 7:00 p.m.
Mid-June to mid-October

Lombard French Market
East St. Charles Rd.,
   (parking lot located on
   former Hammerschmidt
   property, beginning 2005)
Lombard, IL
630.620.5749
Weekly,
Sat 8:00 a.m. to 1:00 p.m.
Early June to late October

Ravinia Farmers Market
Jens Jensen Park
St. John's and Roger Williams
   Aves.
Highland Park, IL
847.432.5570
Weekly,
Wed 7:00 a.m. to 1:00 p.m.
Late June to mid-October

Green Grocers and Health Food Stores

North Side

Andy's Fruit Ranch
4725 N. Kedzie Blvd.
Chicago, IL 60625
773.583.2322
Produce and Hispanic goods market

Arirang Supermarket
4017 W. Lawrence St.
Chicago, IL 60630
773.777.2488
Korean specialty grocery

Armitage Produce
3334 W. Armitage Ave.
Chicago, IL 60647
773.486.8133
Mexican specialty grocery

Bari Foods
1120 W. Grand Ave.
Chicago, IL 60622
312.666.0730
Italian specialty market

Beverly's Natural Health
 Food Store
4434-1/2 N. Damen Ave.
Chicago, IL 60613
773.334.2683
Health food store

California Milwaukee Produce
2633 W. Armitage Ave.
Chicago, IL 60647
773.486.5905
Produce market

Cermak Produce
General grocery
 2820 N. Cicero Ave.
 Chicago, IL 60641
 773.794.1660

4401 W. Armitage Ave.
Chicago, IL 60639
773.227.4700

2701 W. North Ave.
Chicago, IL 60647
773.278.4447

Devon Market
1440 W. Devon Ave.
Chicago, IL 60660
773.338.2572
Multiethnic grocery

Family Fruit Market
4118 N. Cicero Ave.
Chicago, IL 60641
773.481.2500
Produce market

Giselle's
1967 N. Halsted St.
Chicago, IL 60614
312.266.7880
www.gisellesonline.com
Specialty foods and takeout

The Goddess and Grocer
1646 N. Damen Ave.
Chicago, IL 60647
773.342.3200
Specialty foods and takeout

Healing Earth Resources
3111 N. Ashland Ave.
Chicago, IL 60657
773.327.8459
www.healingearthresources.com
Natural products store

J's Vitamins and More
5316 N. Milwaukee Ave.
Chicago, IL 60630
773.763.1917
Health food store

Jimenez
Mexican specialty grocery

  2140 N. Western Ave.
  Chicago, IL 60647
  773.235.0999

  3850 W. Fullerton Ave.
  Chicago, IL 60647
  773.278.6769

La Unica
1515 W. Devon Ave.
Chicago, IL 60660
773.274.7788
Cuban market

Life Spring Health Foods
  and Juice Bar
3178 N. Clark St.
Chicago, IL 60657
773.327.1023
Natural foods store

Makola African Supermarket
1017 W. Wilson St.
Chicago, IL 60640
773.935.6990
African and Caribbean market

New Leaf Grocery
1261 W. Loyola Ave.
Chicago, IL 60626
773.743.0400
www.newleafnatural.net
Health food store

Niko's Produce
2101 N. Milwaukee Ave.
Chicago, IL 60647
773.252.4920
Mexican grocery

Pastoral
2945 N. Broadway St.
Chicago, IL 60657
773.472.4781
Upscale grocery

Sherwyn's
645 W. Diversey Pkwy
Chicago, IL 60614
773.477.1934
www.sherwyns.com
Health food store

Southport Grocery and Cafe
3552 N. Southport Ave.
Chicago, IL 60657
773.665.0100
www.s.portgrocery.com
Specialty food store

Stanley's Fruits and Vegetables
1558 N. Elston Ave.
Chicago, IL 60622
773.276.8050
Organic and conventional
produce market

Trader Joe's
www.traderjoes.com
Specialty grocery

  1840 N. Clybourn Ave.
  Chicago, IL 60614
  312.274.9572

  3745 N. Lincoln Ave.
  Chicago, IL 60613
  773.248.4920

Treasure Island
www.tifoods.com
European grocery

  3460 N. Broadway St.
  Chicago, IL 60657
  773.327.3880

  2121 N. Clybourn Ave.
  Chicago, IL 60614
  773.880.8880

  1639 N. Wells St.
  Chicago, IL 60614
  312.642.1105

Trotter's To Go
1337 W. Fullerton Ave.
Chicago, IL 60614
773.868.6510
www.charlietrotters.com
Specialty foods and takeout

True Nature Foods
6034 N. Broadway St.
Chicago, IL 60660
773.465.6400
Natural foods store

Urban Epicure
1512 W. Berwyn Ave.
Chicago, IL 60640
773.293.3663
www.urbanepicure.com
Specialty foods and takeout

Urban Fridge
2679 N. Lincoln Ave.
Chicago, IL 60614
773.244.6568
www.urbanfridge.com
Specialty foods and takeout

Whole Foods
www.wholefoods.com
Natural and organic food
   grocery

   3300 N. Ashland Ave.
   Chicago, IL 60657
   773.244.4200

   1000 W. North Ave.
   Chicago, IL 60622
   312.587.0648

Downtown
Athens Grocery
324 S. Halsted St.
Chicago, IL 60661
312.454.0940
Greek specialty grocery

Conte de Savoia
1438 W. Taylor St.
Chicago, IL 60607
312.666.3471
Italian specialty grocery

Cyd & D'Pano Chicago
1325 W. Randolph St.
Chicago, IL 60607
312.942.9655
Produce market

Fox & Obel Food Market
401 East Illinois St.
Chicago, IL 60611
312.410.7301
www.fox-obel.com
Gourmet grocery

Kramers Health Foods
230 S. Wabash Ave.
Chicago, IL 60604
312.922.0077
Health food store

Treasure Island
www.tifoods.com
European grocery

   680 N. Lakeshore Dr.
   Chicago, IL 60611
   312.664.0400

   75 W. Elm St.
   Chicago, IL 60610
   312.440.1144

Whole Foods
30 W. Huron St.
Chicago, IL 60610
312.932.9600
www.wholefoods.com
Natural and organic food
   grocery

South Side

Bonne Sante Health Food
1512 E. 53rd St.
Chicago, IL 60615
773.667.5700
Health food store, with
  juice bar

Cermak Produce
3435 S. Archer Ave.
Chicago, IL 60608
773.847.9700
General grocery

Elnora's Health Unlimited
10844 S. Halsted St.
Chicago, IL 60628
773.995.0162
Health food store

Hyde Park Coop
General grocery co-op, with
juice bar

  1226 E. 53rd St.
  Chicago, IL 60615
  773.363.2175

  1526 E. 55th St.
  Chicago, IL 60615
  773.667.1444

La Fruteria
8909 S. Commercial Ave.
Chicago, IL 60617
773.768.4969
African and Caribbean market

Southtown Health Foods
2100 W. 95th St.
Chicago, IL 60643
773.233-1856
Health food store
  with juice bar

Suburban Cook County

A Way of Life
9359 N. Milwaukee Ave.
Niles, IL 60714
847.966.5565
Health food store with
gluten-free specialty

Calabria Imports
13012 S. Western Ave.
Blue Island, IL 60406
708.388.1500
Italian market

Diho Market
6120 W. Dempster St.
Morton Grove, IL 60053
847.965.8688
Chinese grocery

Infinite Light
525 Howard St.
Evanston, IL 60202
847.492.0492
Natural products store

Fruitful Yield
www.fruitfulyield.com
Health products store

  175 W. Golf Rd.
  Schaumburg, IL 60195
  847.882.2999

  5021 W. Oakton St.
  Skokie IL 60077
  847.679.8882

JD Mills Health Foods
635 Chicago Ave.
Evanston, IL 60202
847.491.0940
Natural foods store

Jimenez
Mexican specialty grocery
  5901 W. Roosevelt Rd.
  Cicero, IL 60804
  708.656.6503

GREEN GROCERS

717 Broadway
Melrose Park IL 60106
708.343.3460

550 W. Dundee Ave.
Wheeling, IL 60090
847.229.9295

Mitsuwa
100 E. Algonquin Rd.
Arlington Heights, IL 60005
847.956.6699
www.mitsuwachicago.net
Japanese grocery

New Vitality Health Foods
9177 W. 151st St.
Orland Park IL 60462
708.403.0120
Health food store

Pass Health Foods
7228 W. College Dr.
Palos Heights, IL 60463
708.448.9114
Health food store with
gluten-free specialty

People's Market
1111 Chicago Ave.
Evanston, IL 60202
847.475.9492
Natural and organic food
  grocery

Pita Inn
3910 Dempster St.
Skokie, IL 60076
847.677.0211
Middle Eastern market with
fresh-baked pita bread

South Suburban Co-op
21750 S. Main St.
Matteson, IL 60443
708.747.2256
Natural and organic
  food co-op

Sunset Foods
1127 Church St.
Northbrook, IL 60062
847.272.7700
www.sunsetfoods.com
General grocery

Trader Joe's
www.traderjoes.com
Specialty grocery

17 W. Rand Rd.
Arlington Heights, IL 60004
847.506.0752

1407 Waukegan Rd.
Glenview, IL 60025
847.657.7821

25 N. La Grange Rd.
La Grange, IL 60525
708.579.0838

577 Waukegan Rd.
Northbrook, IL 60062
847.498.9076

14924 S. La Grange Rd.
Orland Park, IL 60462
708.349.9021

Vitality Natural Foods
1100 Central Ave.
Wilmette, IL 60091
847.853.4200
Natural foods store

Whole Foods
www.wholefoods.com
Natural and organic food
  grocery

760 Waukegan Rd.
Deerfield, IL 60015
847.444.1900

1640 Chicago Ave.
Evanston, IL 60201
847.733.1600

1331 N. Rand Rd.
Palatine, IL 60074
847.776.8080

**Collar Counties:
DuPage, Kane, Lake,
McHenry, Will**
All Ways Healthy
123 S. Rand Rd.
Lake Zurich, IL 60047
847.438.9200
www.allwayshealthy.com
Health food store

American Health Foods
5142 W. 95th St.
Oak Lawn, IL 60453
708.423.5099
Health food store

Caputo's Fresh Market
510 W. Lake St.
Addison, IL 606101
630.543.0151
Italian market

Crystal Lake Health
  Food Store
25 East Crystal Lake Ave.
Crystal Lake, IL 60014
815.459.7942
www.clhealth.com
Health food store

Earthly Goods Health
  Foods Inc.
6951 W. Grand Ave.
Gurnee, IL 60031
847.855.9677
www.myearthlygoods.com
Health food store

Fruitful Yield
www.fruitfulyield.com
Health products store

154 S. Bloomingdale Rd.
Bloomingdale, IL 60108
630.894.2553

2129 W. 63rd St.
Downers Grove, IL 60516
630.969.7614

302 S. McLean Blvd.
360 Randall Rd.
S. Elgin IL 60117
847.888.0100

214 N. York Rd.
Elmhurst, IL 60126
630.530.1445

229 W. Roosevelt Rd.
Lombard, IL 60148
630.629.9242

Golden Harvest Health Foods
202 Springhill Rd.
Dundee, IL 60110
847.551.3551
Health food store

Health Plus
210 S. Randall Rd.
Elgin, IL 60123
847.742.8225
Natural foods store

Jimenez
37 York Rd.
Bensenville, IL 60647
630.766.0353
Mexican specialty grocery

Murphy's Health Foods
  and Juice Bar
400 N. Milwaukee Ave.
Libertyville, IL 60048
847.362.4664
Natural foods store

Natural Health Foods Inc.
of Naperville
411 East Ogden Ave.
Naperville IL 60563
630.355.4840
www.shopbydiet.com
Health food store with
gluten-free specialty

Soup to Nuts
716 W. State St.
Geneva, IL 60134
630.232.6646
Health food store

Sunset Foods
www.sunsetfoods.com
General grocery

   1812 Green Bay Rd.
   Highland Park, IL 60035
   847.432.5500

   825 S. Waukegan Rd.
   Lake Forest, IL 60045
   847.234.8380

   1451 W. Peterson
   Libertyville, IL 60048
   847.573.9570

Sweetgrass Market
1742 W. Golf Rd.
Mt. Prospect, IL 60056
847.956.1939
Health food store

Trader Joe's
www.traderjoes.com
Specialty grocery

   1942 W. Fabyan Pkwy #222
   Batavia, IL 60510
   630.879.3234

   122 Ogden Ave.
   Downers Grove, IL 60515
   630.241.1662

   680 Roosevelt Rd.
   Glen Ellyn, IL 60137
   630.858-5077

   44 W. Gartner Rd.
   Naperville, IL 60540
   630.355.4389

   735 W. Main St.
   Lake Zurich, IL 60047
   847.550.7827

Whole Foods
www.wholefoods.com
Natural and organic food
grocery

   7245 W. Lake St.
   River Forest, IL 60305
   708.366.1045

   151 Rice Lake Square
   Wheaton, IL 60187
   630.588.1500

   201 W. 63rd St.
   Willowbrook, IL 60514
   630.655.5000

Wild Oats Market
500 East Ogden Ave.
Hinsdale, IL 60521
630.986.8500
www.wildoats.com
Natural and organic food
grocery

Alphabetical Index

A La Carte, 136
A La Turka: Turkish Kitchen, 14
Abhiruchi, 15
Addis Abeba, 16
Alice and Friends' Vegetarian Café, 17
Amarind's, 18
Ambria, 19
Amitabul, 20
Amrit Ganga, 21
Anatolian Kabob, 22
Andies, 23
Annapurna Fast Food, 24
Arbor Vitae Java and Juice, 160
Artopolis Bakery, Café, and Agora, 86
Arya Bhavan, 25
Asiana, 26
Atomix, 27

bd's mongolian barbeque, 28, 161
Bialy Café, 87
Bite Café, 29
Blind Faith Café, 137
Buzz Café, 138
BUZZ, The, 139

Café Ennui, 30
Caffe de Lucca, 31
Cedars Mediterranean Kitchen, 120
Chicago Diner, 32
Chowpatti Vegetarian Restaurant, 140
Cousin's, 33
Crofton on Wells, 88

Da'Nali's, 141
Desert Rose Café, 34
Dharma Garden Thai Cuisine, 35

Earwax Café, 36
El Faro, 121
El Tinajon, 37
Emerald City, The, 38
Ethio Café, 39
Ex Libris Coffee Shop, 122

Fitness Café, 142, 162
Flat Top Grill, 40, 89, 143
Flo, 90
Flying Saucer, 41
Foodlife, 91
Fresh Choice, 42, 92
Frullati Café, 163

Gaylord India, 93
Gioco, 94
Great American Bagel, 144
Green Zebra, 95

Handlebar Bar and Grill, 43
Hashalom, 44
Heartland Café, 45
Hema's Kitchen, 46

I.C.Y. Vegetarian Restaurant and Juice Bar, 123
India House, 96, 145

Jal Hind, 47
Jalapeno's, 164
Jane's, 48
Jim's Grill, 49
Jinx Café, 50
John's Place, 51
Joy Yee's Noodle Shop, 124, 146
Jubilee Juice, 97

Kabul House, 52, 147
Karyn's Bistro, 53
Katerina's, 54
Khyber Pass, 148
Klay Oven, 98

Kopi: A Traveler's Café, 55

Leona's, 56, 99, 125, 149
Letizia's Natural Bakery, 57
Little Egypt, 150
Lo Cal Zone, 100
Lovitt, 58
Lula Café, 59

M. Henry, 60
Mac Kelly's Greens and Things, 101
Mama Desta's Red Sea Restaurant, 61
Mellow Yellow, 126
Moti Mahal, 62
Mt. Everest Restaurant, 151
Mysore Woodlands, 63, 165

Natural Harvest, A, 127
Nile, The, 128
Noodles and Company, 152, 166

Oasis Café, 102
Old Jerusalem, 103
Orange, 64, 104

Pacific Café, 65
PapaSpiros Greek Taverna, 153
Pasta Bowl, The, 66
Pegasus, 105
Phoenix Restaurant and Phoenix Noodle and Dumpling House, 129
Pick Me Up Café, 67
Pili Pili, 106
Privata, 107

Rajun Cajun, 130
Ras Dashen, 68
Reza's, 69, 108
Riques Regional Mexican Food, 70
Roly Poly Sandwiches, 167
Rose Angelis, 71
Royal Thai, 72
Russian Tea Time, 109

Salad Spinners, 110
Sangria Restaurant and Tapas Bar, 111
Sayat Nova, 112
Sher-a Punjab Restaurant, 73
Siam Noodle and Rice, 74
Slice of Life, 154
Soul Vegetarian East, 131
Southtown Health Foods, 132
Sri Ganesh, 168
Star of Siam, 113
Sultan's Market, 75
Swagat Indian Cuisine, 169
Sweet Tomatoes, 155, 170
Szechuan Garden, 76

Taste of Lebanon, 77
Tel Aviv Kosher Pizza, 78
Thai Spice, 171
Thyme and Honey Restaurant and Lounge, 156
Tiffin, the Indian Kitchen, 79
Tizi Melloul, 114
Tokyo Lunchbox, 115

Udupi Palace, 80, 157
Uncommon Ground Coffeehouse and Café, 81
Unique So Chique, 82
U.S. Cellular Field, 133

Vegetarian Fun Foods Supreme, 134
Vermilion, 116
Victory's Banner, 83
Vitality Natural Foods, 158

Yes Thai, 84
Yummy Bowl, 172

Zealous, 117

ALPHABETICAL INDEX

Cuisine Index

Afghan
Kabul House, 52, 147

American
Bialy Cafe, 87
Café Ennui, 30
Crofton on Wells, 88
Da'Nali's, 141
Earwax Cafe, 36
Green Zebra, 95
Heartland Cafe, 45
Jane's, 48
Jinx Cafe, 50
Leona's, 99
Lovitt, 58
M. Henry, 60
Mac Kelly's Greens and Things, 101
Mellow Yellow, 126
Pick Me Up Cafe, 67
Roly Poly Sandwiches, 167
Salad Spinners, 110
Sweet Tomatoes, 155, 170
U.S. Cellular Field, 133
Zealous, 117

Armenian
Sayat Nova, 112

Asian
Alice and Friends' Vegetarian Café, 17

Buddhist
Amitabul, 20

Chinese
Phoenix Restaurant and Phoenix Noodle and Dumpling House, 129
Szechuan Garden, 76
Yummy Bowl, 172

Ethiopian
Addis Abeba, 16
Ethio Cafe, 39
Mama Desta's Red Sea Restaurant, 61
Ras Dashen, 68

French
Ambria, 19
Pili Pili, 106

Greek
Andies, 23
Artopolis Bakery, Café, and Agora, 86
PapaSpiros Greek Taverna, 153
Pegasus, 105

Guatemalan
El Tinajon, 37

Indian
Abhiruchi, 15
Amrit Ganga, 21
Annapurna Fast Food, 24
Arya Bhavan, 25
Gaylord India, 93
Hema's Kitchen, 46
India House, 96, 145
Jal Hind, 47
Khyber Pass, 148
Klay Oven, 98
Moti Mahal, 62
Mt. Everest Restaurant, 151
Mysore Woodlands, 63, 165
Rajun Cajun, 130
Sher-a-Punjab Restaurant, 73
Sri Ganesh, 168
Swagat Indian Cuisine, 169
Tiffin, the Indian Kitchen, 79
Udupi Palace, 80, 157
Vermilion, 116

Israeli
Hashalom, 44

Italian
Caffe de Lucca, 31
Da'Nali's, 141
Gioco, 94
Leona's, 56, 99, 125, 149
Pasta Bowl, The, 66
Privata, 107
Rose Angelis, 71

Japanese
Tokyo Lunchbox, 115

Juice Bar
Southtown Health Foods, 132

Korean
Amitabul, 20
Jim's Grill, 49

Latin American
Vermilion, 116

Lebanese
Andies, 23

Mediterranean
Anatolian Kabob, 22
Cedars Mediterranean Kitchen, 120
Cousin's, 33
Katerina's, 54
Little Egypt, 150
Reza's, 69, 108
Tizi Melloul, 114

Mexican
Bialy Cafe, 87
El Faro, 121
Jalapeno's, 164
Privata, 107
Riques Regional Mexican Food, 70

Middle Eastern
Desert Rose Café, 34
Emerald City, The, 38
Oasis Cafe, 102
Old Jerusalem, 103
Sultan's Market, 75
Taste of Lebanon, 77
The Nile, 128

Moroccan
Hashalom, 44

Multiethnic
A La Carte, 136
Arbor Vitae Java and Juice, 160
Atomix, 27
Bite Cafe, 29
Blind Faith Cafe, 137
Buzz Cafe, 138
BUZZ, The, 139
Chicago Diner, 32
Chowpatti Vegetarian Restaurant, 140
Da'Nali's, 141
Ex Libris Coffee Shop, 122
Fitness Cafe, 142, 162
Flying Saucer, 41
Foodlife, 91
Fresh Choice, 42, 92
Great American Bagel, 144
Handlebar Bar and Grill, 43
I.C.Y. Vegetarian Restaurant and Juice Bar, 123
John's Place, 51
Jubilee Juice, 97
Kopi: A Traveler's Cafe, 55
Letizia's Natural Bakery, 57
Lo Cal Zone, 100
Lula Cafe, 59
Natural Harvest, A, 127
Noodles and Company, 152, 166
Orange, 64, 104

Slice of Life, 154
Tel Aviv Kosher Pizza, 78
Thyme and Honey Restaurant and Lounge, 156
Uncommon Ground Coffeehouse and Cafe, 81
Unique So Chique, 82
Vegetarian Fun Foods Supreme, 134
Victory's Banner, 83
Vitality Natural Foods, 158

Nepali
Mt. Everest Restaurant, 151

New Mexican
Flo, 90

Pakistani
Hema's Kitchen, 46
Tiffin, the Indian Kitchen, 79

Pan-Asian
bd's mongolian barbeque, 28, 161
Dharma Garden Thai Cuisine, 35
Flat Top Grill, 40, 89, 143
Joy Yee's Noodle Shop, 124, 146
Pacific Cafe, 65

Raw
Karyn's Bistro, 53

Russian
Russian Tea Time, 109

Smoothies
Frullati Café, 163

Soul Food
Rajun Cajun, 130
Soul Vegetarian East, 131

Spanish
Sangria Restaurant and Tapas Bar, 111

Thai
Amarind's, 18
Dharma Garden Thai Cuisine, 35
Royal Thai, 72
Siam Noodle and Rice, 74
Star of Siam, 113
Thai Spice, 171
Yes Thai, 84
Yummy Bowl, 172

Turkish
A La Turka: Turkish Kitchen, 14
Anatolian Kabob, 22
Cousin's, 33

Vietnamese
Asiana, 26

CUISINE INDEX

Top 10 Index

The following top ten lists are in alphabetical order.

Top 10 for Food
1. Blind Faith, 137
2. Crofton on Wells, 88
3. Green Zebra, 95
4. Hema's Kitchen, 46
5. Lula Cafe, 59
6. Soul Vegetarian East, 131
7. Sri Ganesh, 168
8. Tizi Melloul, 114
9. Vermilion, 116
10. Zealous, 117

Top 10 for Atmosphere
1. Ambria, 19
2. Buzz Cafe, 138
3. Caffe de Lucca, 31
4. Dharma Garden Thai Cuisine, 35
5. Earwax Cafe, 36
6. Karyn's Bistro, 53
7. M. Henry, 60
8. Ras Dashen, 68
9. Unique So Chique, 82
10. Victory's Banner, 83

Top 10 Best Buys
1. Amrit Ganga, 21
2. Anatolian Kabob, 22
3. El Faro, 121
4. Jal Hind, 47
5. Little Egypt, 150
6. Rose Angelis, 71
7. Siam Noodle and Rice, 74
8. Taste of Lebanon, 77
9. Tel Aviv Kosher Pizza, 78
10. Vegetarian Fun Foods Supreme, 134

Other VegOut Vegetarian Guides® from Gibbs Smith, Publisher

Vegetarian Guide® to New York City
by Justin Schwartz
1-58685-382-1

Vegetarian Guide® to Southern California
by Kathy Lynn Siegel
1-58685-265-5

Vegetarian Guide® to Washington, D.C.
by Andrew Evans
1-58685-471-2

Vegetarian Guide® to San Francisco Bay Area
by Michele Anna Jordan
1-58685-383-X

Vegetarian Guide® to Seattle & Portland
by George Stevenson
1-58685-441-0

Vegetarian Guide® to Denver & Salt Lake City
by Andrea Mather
1-58685-389-9

AVAILABLE AT YOUR LOCAL BOOKSTORE, AT WWW.VEGOUTGUIDE.COM, OR BY CALLING 1.800.748.5439

Gibbs Smith, Publisher